MANAGING DIFFICULT STAFF

To
Miss B Lund
sometime teacher
Camm's School, Eckington

MANAGING DIFFICULT STAFF

Effective Procedures and the Law

Helga Drummond

**KOGAN
PAGE**

Disclaimers

While every care has been taken to ensure the accuracy of the contents, readers should note that changes occur frequently in employment legislation and case law. Readers are advised, therefore, when disciplinary matters occasion it, always to seek independent legal advice.

All cases described here are based on real incidents. However, in order to protect the identity of those involved, all names, and certain other details, have been changed. No resemblance to any person, living or dead, is intended.

First published in 1990

Kogan Page Limited
120 Pentonville Road
London N1 9JN

© Helga Drummond, 1990

British Library Cataloguing in Publication Data

A CIP record for this book is available from the British Library.

ISBN 0-7494-0136-2

Typeset by DP Photosetting, Aylesbury, Bucks
Printed and bound in Great Britain by
Richard Clay Ltd, Bungay, Suffolk

Contents

Acknowledgements

This book reflects many years' work in personnel and industrial relations. I am grateful to all my colleagues for sharing their ideas and experience. My thinking has been heavily influenced by the period of my career spent in the former Industrial Relations Unit of Bradford City Council. I wish to thank all my former colleagues there, notably Steve Cook, Bill Henry, Barry Jacobs and Steve Reiss for their example of professional excellence, and for their friendship and support. I am especially grateful to Bernard McEvoy, whose talent as a practitioner and his willingness to explain, were inspiring. I also owe much to Paul Lowenberg, Director of Works of Manchester City Council for his legal and analytical insights. Finally, and by no means least, I thank Elizabeth Chell for encouraging me to write.

Preface

Applying disciplinary procedures is one of the most difficult aspects of a manager's or personnel officer's role. It is an area surrounded by legal complexity and one which is often emotionally charged concerning as it does a sensitive element of employee relations. Managers strive to behave in a manner consistent with good practice, often only too aware that not only is an employee's livelihood at stake, but that their own judgement and credibility are also on trial.

This book aims to meet the need for a single, comprehensive and readable volume containing both legal information and practical guidance. It addresses a host of questions and problems such as:

- 'He says he won't do it because it's not in his job description ...'

- 'He seemed all right at interview. Now I've discovered the police have a file on him. What shall I do?'

- 'He's been like that for years. The trade union says it's too late to discipline him ...'

- 'The cook's drunk, can I send her home? What if she won't go?'

- 'I've received an anonymous letter ...'

The structure of this book

The text is basically divided into two parts. The first part of the book deals with the various types of misconduct including dishonesty, poor performance, conduct outside work and insubordination. Each chapter begins with an outline of the legal background and then examines specific cases and advises on how to approach them. Considerable attention is devoted to complex and ambiguous examples as it is these which cause greatest difficulty, for example:

A group of slaters discovered that one of their colleagues had hepatitis B. Despite a medical officer's assurance that there was no risk of anyone contracting the disease, the foreman cordoned off the man's work area with red tape and told the rest of the gang not to work with him.

A theme of the book is that conflict can be reduced and time saved if discipline is 'managed' in the same way that other aspects of organisations such as production are managed. Consequently emphasis is placed upon preventing situations escalating to a point where disciplinary action becomes the only option. This includes advice on effective communications and training and on how managers can exert their authority without causing upset. It is also stressed that disciplinary offences are often symptomatic of managerial weaknesses. Examples are analysed with advice on how to improve systems and practices.

The book opens with a résumé of the law concerning disciplinary hearings and dismissals. This is essential reading as it explains concepts such as natural justice and constructive dismissal which are referred to in subsequent chapters. The law pertaining to strikes and other forms of industrial action is a topic in its own right and outside the scope of this book which is concerned with individual behaviour.

The next six chapters are devoted to the most common categories of serious misconduct. Chapter Two concerns dishonesty and examines some of the difficulties in dealing with theft and how to overcome these. Much emphasis is placed upon the importance of investigating before calling the police and upon the different standards of proof applicable to disciplinary hearings and court proceedings respectively. The chapter closes with a discussion on security in organisations.

Chapter Three provides a framework for dealing with performance problems. The approach is highly analytical, stressing the need for clarity and objectivity in specifying standards and measuring results. Chapter Four explains how the model developed in the previous chapter can be applied in practice. Professional and managerial performance is covered in some detail.

Chapter Five is devoted to disobedience. While it is made clear that employees must obey their employer, the emphasis is upon conflict management and the prevention of escalation.

Chapter Six examines other forms of serious misconduct including violence and violation of health and safety regulations, damage to property and so forth. Chapter Seven, entitled 'Dismissal for "Some

Other Substantial Reason"', is virtually a continuation of the previous chapter. This includes sections on imprisonment, sexual harassment, employee competition and conduct outside work.

The second part of the book is devoted to preparing for a disciplinary hearing or an industrial tribunal. Although many books and journal articles stress the need for thorough preparation, few describe what this means in practice or how to set about it. This book explains in detail how to conduct a management investigation, compile statements, cross-examine witnesses and so forth.

Chapter Eight is devoted to suspension. It contains advice on when to suspend, when not to suspend, and how to go about suspending someone.

Chapter Nine explains why it is so important to investigate before even contemplating disciplinary proceedings. Chapter Ten then describes the preparation necessary to conduct an effective investigation. Chapter Eleven advises upon investigating documentary evidence and detecting fraud.

Chapter Twelve describes how to conduct an investigatory interview and compile statements. It answers questions such as:

- What if an employee refuses to give a statement?

- What if a member of the public is involved?

- What if an employee confesses and then retracts?

This chapter is based on police practice. If the recommendations seem pedantic or overly elaborate, it should be noted that the majority of cases which founder, do so because of inadequate investigation. The guidelines set out in this chapter are tried and tested. Used properly, they do work.

Chapter Thirteen explains how to prepare a case for presentation at a disciplinary hearing while Chapter Fourteen advises upon advocacy. Both chapters stress the importance of easing the listener's task. Presenters are urged to rehearse and redraft their work to achieve a lucid and succinct performance. Advice on the purpose and pitfalls of cross-examination and re-examination is also included.

Chapter Fifteen concerns the disciplinary hearing itself. It explains how to organise and control a hearing and how to recognise particular defence tactics. A model for systematic and objective appraisal of evidence and decision making is described.

The book closes with advice on defending cases at industrial tribunal. The brevity of the chapter reflects the fact that most of the relevant points have already been covered in previous chapters while the details of tribunal procedure are outside the scope of this book. It is hoped nonetheless that the information will provide useful, if basic, guidance.

Furthermore, it is no exaggeration to suggest that *applying the recommendations contained in this book, substantially reduces the likelihood of appearing before a tribunal*. If procedures are correctly applied, employees will see that their case has little prospect of succeeding.

Who should use this book

The cases and examples contained within the text are drawn from a variety of organisations and a variety of job levels. These include the professions and senior management as well as blue-collar staff. It is hoped therefore that the book will be useful not only to those working in industry but also those employed in the public sector including local government, the health service and in education.

In addition to general managers, it is hoped that the book will prove relevant to personnel professionals, especially those with limited experience. Those studying personnel management on degree and professional courses may also find it useful.

Using this book effectively

Although this book has been designed for easy reference, readers are advised to read the whole text at least once and to refresh themselves periodically. Those wishing to obtain a quick overview are directed to Chapters One and Nine, together with the introduction to each chapter and its concluding summary and checklist.

Anyone directly involved in disciplinary proceedings is advised to consult the relevant section and any related material before acting. A few minutes spent refreshing one's memory can save many hours of wasted effort. The least effective time to begin reading is when Form IT3, the summons to appear before an industrial tribunal, arrives!

To facilitate easy reference, as far as possible each chapter is complete in itself. Some repetition is therefore necessary. It is hoped that readers will not be offended by the predominance of the masculine form.

Using this book for teaching

The case material has two purposes. First, it serves to illustrate the application of legal principles to complex examples. Second, it is intended to stimulate thought and reasoning by giving the reader an opportunity to test his own conclusions. Almost all of the cases lend themselves to classroom discussion and analysis.

Part One
The Law and Misconduct

Introduction

Before 1975, there was little to prevent an employee from being sacked at will and without warning. The Employment Protection Act 1975, and latterly the Employment Consolidation Act (EPCA) 1978, changed this dramatically by giving nearly all dismissed employees with more than two full years of continuous service, the right to complain to an industrial tribunal.

The role of the tribunal is to decide whether dismissal was reasonable 'having regard to equity and the substantial merits of the case' (EPCA 1978). The full meaning of this is explained elsewhere in this book. Here it is sufficient to note that the employer must prove that:

- Dismissal was based upon a fair and thorough investigation.

- Correct procedures were observed and proceedings were conducted in accordance with natural justice.

- The decision was a reasonable one given all the circumstances.

Proving fair dismissal has become more rigorous since 1986. Up until then, employers could rely upon the so called 'no difference rule'. For example, failure to inform an employee of his rights to representation or to specify allegations precisely would not harm the employer's case if he could show that even had proper procedures been followed, the outcome would have been the same.

The House of Lords' ruling in the *Polkey* case (*Polkey* v *Drayton* AC 344), revoked the 'no difference rule'. Consequently dismissal can now be overturned on procedural grounds alone. This means for instance, that instant dismissal for stealing will be unfair even if the employee is caught red-handed. This is because the employer's hasty action has deprived the employee of the *opportunity* to explain.

Correct observance of procedures requires:

- a working knowledge of legislation; and

- the ability to apply legal principles to individual cases.

The first of these requirements is less daunting than it may sound. Although unfair dismissal is surrounded by a plethora of case law, for day-to-day purposes, a grasp of a few basic principles will suffice.

Legal knowledge alone, however, is insufficient. Managers and personnel officers must be able to analyse individual cases to identify the substantive issues in order that the law may be properly applied. Effective analysis requires the ability to approach problems:

- systematically;

- objectively;

- critically.

Systematically means to order and work through often copious and confused verbal accounts and documentation to extract and summarise the relevant issues. *Objectively* means to carry out this task without being influenced by prejudice and emotions. *Critically* means to question other people's definitions of reality, and, where appropriate, to re-define problems and issues clearly and precisely.

Managing discipline

Although important, legal and analytical knowledge and skills are only secondary. Indeed, where discipline is properly managed, procedures are virtually redundant in that most problems are resolved long before the possibility of formal action arises.

Despite the value of control strategies however, discipline is seldom accorded the same managerial attention as is, say, accounting and production. Enforcing standards is commonly regarded with distaste. This may reflect the repressive connotation of the word 'discipline' which is synonymous with punishment, humiliation and coercion.

The constructive aspects of managing discipline are generally under-emphasised. For example, it is seldom acknowledged that employees rely upon management to maintain order within the work environment and to control those who might otherwise be disruptive or destructive. Discipline protects individuals from the worst effects of the informal organisation. Moreover, enforcing standards reduces feelings of injustice such as: 'So and so doesn't pull his weight ... Such and such gets her own way all the time ... It's not fair, it's time someone did something about him.'

Whereas anarchy destroys morale, research has suggested that fair and properly administered sanctions actually enhance employee commitment.* This supports the theories of the French sociologist Durkheim who argued that people feel more secure working within clearly defined boundaries than to be given total discretion. In other words, the maintenance of discipline may be viewed as an essential element of communication whereby the organisation's expectations can be clearly understood and enforced.

The need for procedures

Although formal disciplinary procedures are a last resort, it is equally important that they are used where necessary. A common reason for reluctance to invoke procedure is fear of industrial action. This is understandable but seldom well founded. Exceptionally, an inexperienced union representative might behave obstreperously or uncooperatively. Overall, however, trade unions accept the need for organisations to regulate standards and behaviour. Disciplinary procedures are regarded as legitimate mechanisms for this purpose. This explains why these are often jointly agreed between management and the trade unions and also the fact that the facility of a disciplinary hearing is a contractual right.

Obviously trade unions have a responsibility to defend their members at hearings, and may do so vigorously. On the other hand, officials represent many employees. They often operate under pressure and can ill afford to over-react or to pursue a hopeless case on behalf of an individual. Therefore, while a trade union representative will do his best for an employee, provided the decision is fair, and procedures are observed, the outcome will normally be accepted.

Indeed, many trade union officials will say that more problems are caused by circumnavigation of disciplinary procedures than the reverse. As they see it, instead of discussing their concerns openly, managers resort to innuendo and manipulation. These only result in feelings of victimisation and distrust. Unpleasant though a disciplinary hearing may be, it at least enables an employee to know where he stands and to defend himself, rather than be forever condemned sinisterly and secretly.

Another reason for some managers' reluctance to invoke procedures, is the potential aftermath of hostility and embarrassment. This is a valid

* eg, Arvey, R. D. and Jones, A. P. 'The use of discipline in organisational settings: a framework for future research', in L. L. Cummins and B. Staw (eds) 1985 *Research in Organization Behavior*, Vol 7, JAI Press, London.

but one-sided concern in that it fails to take account of the advantages of dealing with discipline in procedure which are that:

- it sets the issue in perspective;

- the outcome is predictable; and

- it signals a clear end to the matter.

Potential disciplinary matters frequently lend themselves to rumour and exaggeration. Conversely, formal action can only be based upon tangible facts capable of substantiation. These are usually considerably less sensational than informal networks might suggest.

Since disciplinary procedures specify the range of responses open to the employer, the employee can predict the outcome to within only a few possibilities which helps reduce fear and distrust. It may even be easier for him to reconcile himself to the certainty of dismissal than to the fear of being obliquely demoted or suffering some similar loss of power or status.

Once the process is concluded, the issue is at an end. The employee knows what he must do (or not do) to avoid further sanctions. Provided he complies, he need have nothing further to worry about. This is surely preferable to continuing uncertainty.

Finally, it is emphasised that managers are responsible for the conduct and performance of their subordinates. If they fail to manage and to intervene where necessary and in the appropriate manner, ultimately they may find themselves sanctioned. A right to manage implies a duty to manage.

Chapter One
The Legal Background to Disciplinary Hearings and Dismissals

Introduction

This chapter summarises and explains the law concerning the conduct of disciplinary proceedings. This is necessary in order to set the stage for the following chapters which concentrate upon the practical aspects of dealing with conduct and performance including conducting management investigations, disciplinary hearings and internal appeals.

An employee who has been dismissed (with or without notice) is entitled to bring an unfair dismissal claim before an industrial tribunal, providing he has two years' continuous service with his employer. The role of a tribunal is to decide whether the employer has acted reasonably in treating the matter as sufficient reason for dismissal, 'Having regard to equity and the substantial merits of the case' (s. 57 (3) Employment Protection Consolidation Act 1978). The meaning of this will unfold as this chapter proceeds. Here it is sufficient to note that the tribunal will take into account the extent to which the employer's actions are consistent with the Advisory Conciliation and Arbitration Service (ACAS) Code of Practice on discipline. This has a similar status to that of the Highway Code, that is, it is not compulsory *per se* but failure to observe it may lead to a conclusion of unfair dismissal. ACAS have now supplemented the code with a free advisory handbook.* The reference to both documents throughout this chapter reflects their quasi-legal significance.

* *Discipline at Work* (1987), the ACAS advisory handbook. This is a general guide on how to interpret the ACAS Code of Practice on Disciplinary Practices and Procedures at Work. Both publications are available free from any ACAS office, the handbook actually contains a copy of the code.

Although tribunals are intended to operate with the minimum of formality, in practice the process is exacting and legal representation of parties is by no means unusual. Either side may appeal to the Employment Appeals Tribunal (EAT) on points of law. Further levels of appeal up to the House of Lords exist. It is important to appreciate that anything associated with the disciplinary process — informal conversations, file notes, even hearsay — is potentially admissable as evidence and, therefore, open to judicial and public scrutiny. Consequently, much stress is placed in this book upon the need for correct recording and documenting at all stages.

An adverse judgement is potentially expensive and embarrassing as proceedings are normally held in public and reported. For example, an Employment Appeals Tribunal said of one employer:

> In a nutshell (and putting the most charitable interpretation on the facts from the employer's point of view) this is a case of a small employee being crushed by a stunning ineptitude and lack of foresight or understanding of what decisions taken in London mean to a £100 a week clerk in a branch in the provinces. If that were not the case, and if the negative attitude and response of the bank were deliberate, then they were the actions of a callous and indifferent employer consciously seeking to drive out from its employment an employee without wishing to compensate him in any way by way of redundancy or otherwise (*United Bank* v *Akhtar*, Industrial Relations Law Reports 5, 1989).

Natural justice

All disciplinary proceedings must be consistent with the three rules of natural justice. These are unwritten but commonly expressed as follows:

- The employee must know the full case against him.

- The employee must be given an opportunity to explain.

- Those conducting the hearing must be impartial.

Each of these rules is explained below.

Informing an employee of the case against him

This means that the employee must be informed of everything of which he is accused. Allegations must, therefore, be precise, and the employee must hear all of the evidence forming the basis of the employer's suspicion. This implies that in complex cases, the employee has time to assimilate documentary evidence and any other information to be brought against him.

Affording an opportunity to explain

Prior to the issue of a warning or dismissal, the employee must be afforded an opportunity to explain or to offer a statement in mitigation. This also implies that the employee must be able to challenge management's evidence and to produce his own. The person hearing the case must act reasonably in judging the relevance of the employee's evidence. Reasonableness in this context means:

- listening attentively to what is said;

- making an impartial assessment based on the balance of probability; and

- explaining whether and to what extent, the employee's evidence is accepted and why.

The disciplinary hearing is the mechanism whereby the employee has the opportunity to state his case. If he fails to avail himself of it, for example by failing to attend the hearing, dismissal is fair, provided the employee knows this is a potential consequence. The employee's representative however, can stand surrogate. Natural justice is satisfied if the employee's representative hears the evidence and has the opportunity to respond on the employee's behalf. The employee need not say anything or even attend the hearing.

A comprehensive management investigation is essential, regardless of the employee's right to produce evidence. Comprehensive means that the employer should consider contrary or mitigating facts and information. He must not rely upon the employee to articulate these at the hearing.

The employee's explanation must be heard personally by the person empowered to dismiss. It is inadmissible for the person presenting the case to relay the employee's account. Even where an employee admits to an offence, a hearing is still necessary to give him the opportunity to offer a statement in mitigation or explain why dismissal or a particular level of warning is inappropriate. This applies no matter how serious the offence.

The requirements of impartiality

The person hearing the case must be unbiased. Bias is defined as holding an adverse view or prejudging the issue. The person hearing the case, therefore, should have had no prior involvement. Since justice must not only be done, but be seen to be done, the mere appearance of bias may violate the rules of natural justice. Bias may be inferred for instance, if the person hearing the case is seen talking to the management side before the hearing commences. It is immaterial that the meeting is unconnected with the hearing; the mere fact that it occurred appears suspicious.

Constructive dismissal and resignation

Constructive dismissal

The relationship of trust and confidence between employer and employee must be mutual. Constructive dismissal arises where the employer destroys the employee's trust by breaching, or intending to breach, a fundamental contractual term. Examples include: refusal to pay; unilateral alteration of job content; failure to investigate allegations of sexual harassment; removal of a company car; and requiring someone to work at another location where there is no express or implied contractual term permitting it. Arbitrary or unreasonable enforcement of contractual terms such as an order to relocate without reasonable notice may also be tantamount to constructive dismissal. The employee is entitled to leave with or without giving notice but the breach must be sufficiently serious to entitle him to leave immediately. Within the context of workplace discipline, constructive dismissal occurs, for example, where the penalty is disproportionate to the offence or a penalty not permitted by the employee's contract is imposed. Constructive dismissal may be retracted but only before the employee explicitly accepts it and leaves.

Resignation

In law, resignation may be for any reason or for none. It is important to ascertain that an employee really wishes to resign before treating him as having done so. For instance, an employee who loses his temper and storms out of the workplace, vowing never to return, should not immediately be regarded as having resigned. The law accepts that we are all human and capable of acting hastily, and that we do not always mean what we say. This does not, of course, preclude warning the employee about his misconduct when he returns.

Advising an employee to resign or discussing the possibility of his leaving the organisation is not, by itself, tantamount to constructive dismissal. While it should always be made clear that dismissal is a possible outcome of proceedings, 'resign or else' threats however, will almost certainly be regarded as constructive dismissal. Circumspection is therefore advisable as the discussion may easily be misinterpreted, either innocently or deliberately.

Employers are not obliged to accept an employee's resignation. In the public sector for example, it is sometimes felt necessary to pursue disciplinary proceedings in order to restore confidence in the organisation. The employee continues to be paid until disciplinary proceedings are concluded. It is immaterial whether he appears at the hearing or not; the point has been made.

Achieving fairness

Prior to the hearing

Where disciplinary action is contemplated, fairness requires that:

- proceedings are instigated promptly; and
- the employee is informed of his rights.

A disciplinary hearing must be called as soon as practicable. An employee must either be informed that an investigation is taking place in order to enable him to preserve his recollections, or that disciplinary proceedings are being contemplated. The exception to this is where secrecy is essential to avoid premature disclosure of suspicion, for instance, where surveillance is necessary.

The employee must, however, be in a fit state to respond to an investigation or hearing. If necessary, proceedings should be postponed to allow him to compose himself. Furthermore, the timescale must allow the employee a reasonable period in which to take advice, arrange representation and prepare his defence.

The employee is entitled to be informed of the date, time and place of the hearing and of his rights to trade union representation or to be accompanied by a friend. If dismissal is a potential outcome of proceedings, this should be made clear. The status of all meetings should be explained to the employee. A management interview is separate and distinct from a disciplinary hearing and should never be converted into one.

The disciplinary hearing

The purposes of a disciplinary hearing are:

- to establish whether reasonable grounds exist for a belief in the employee's guilt; and
- to determine what penalty, if any, is appropriate.

Fairness requires that:

1. The person hearing the case must be independent.

2. Evidence against the employee must be presented in full.
3. Sanctions must only be applied on the basis of adequate evidence.

Independent means that the person hearing the case should not have been concerned with the investigation nor should he be a witness. This does not mean, however, that he need approach the case from a standpoint of total ignorance. It is quite acceptable for the person hearing the case to form a preliminary view, *provided* he does not make up his mind beforehand. An informed mind is not necessarily a biased one.

The employee is entitled to hear everything against him. The person presenting the case should therefore explain not only the allegations but should detail in full the management evidence in order to give the employee a reasonable opportunity of challenging it.

It is unfair to act upon inadequate evidence. No hard and fast rules exist over the admissability of evidence and it is, therefore, a matter of judgement as to what is or is not adequate. Generally speaking, information must be reasonably reliable, and its reliability must be taken into account.

Conflicting evidence requires judgement by the person hearing the case. It is unnecessary for the employee's guilt to be proven beyond reasonable doubt. A reasonable conclusion based on the balance of probabilities is acceptable, provided a reasonable investigation has taken place. *Balance of probabilities means more probable than not.* Police evidence may be used, even if it would be rejected by the courts. Being charged by the police, however, does not amount to evidence. Conversely, court acquittal does not automatically invalidate disciplinary proceedings.

Representation

No legal right to trade union representation exists unless provided for in the employee's contract of employment. The ACAS Code of Practice on discipline, however, states that employees should be allowed a trade union official or colleague to represent them regardless of whether procedures provide for such representation. An employer may insist that a trade union representative belong to a recognised trade union, failing which, a colleague may attend as representative.

Trade union officials are bound by the same rules and standards of conduct as other employees. Where, however, disciplinary proceedings are contemplated against a union official, the full-time trade union representative must be notified.

In law, disciplinary proceedings are regarded as private discussions between employer and employee. Employees are not entitled to legal representation either during the course of a managerial investigation or at a disciplinary hearing or internal appeal. An employee may therefore be instructed to participate in any of the foregoing processes without the presence of a solicitor or barrister. The only circumstances where legal representation may be appropriate are where criminal proceedings are contemplated or where the employer is legally represented.

Employees whose command of English is limited, or who are deaf or dumb, should be allowed an interpreter in addition to colleague or trade union representation unless the interpreter also acts in this capacity.

Deciding an appropriate penalty

What does 'reasonable' mean?

The law requires employers to respond reasonably to disciplinary matters. Reasonableness in this context requires the employer to weight:

- the gravity of the offence;
- the employee's length of service;
- the employee's previous record;
- the organisation's rules; and
- previous responses to similar cases.

The ACAS handbook recommends that:

1. Employees committing minor offences should receive a formal oral warning and be informed that a note will be retained for reference.
2. More serious offences or a succession of minor offences should be met with a formal written warning.
3. A final warning, or other penalty such as demotion or suspension without pay if the employee's contract provides for it, is reasonable where the employee has received a previous warning.
4. Where an employee's conduct is not sufficiently serious to warrant dismissal but is sufficiently serious to warrant only one warning, the warning may be first and final.
5. If all previous stages are exhausted, dismissal with notice is the final step.
6. Employees committing gross misconduct may be dismissed without being warned and without notice.

The employer is required to demonstrate that there was good reason for dismissal. Dismissal for a first offence is justifiable only for gross misconduct or 'some other substantial reason' as termed in law. Gross misconduct is defined as conduct sufficiently serious as to entitle the employer to terminate employment without notice, that is, dishonesty, disobedience or 'Some other substantial reason' (SOSR). The latter means just what it says, ie, some reason sufficiently serious to warrant dismissal in view of the position the employee held.

Warnings

The rules of natural justice and the foregoing points apply to warnings in the same way that they apply to dismissals. A warning should be precise, clear, and should emphasise the consequences of further misconduct. These comments apply with particular force to final warnings as dismissal may follow for even a minor subsequent transgression. Final warnings should indicate that no further warnings will be given.

ACAS recommends that warnings be expunged after a period of good conduct ranging from 6 to 12 months depending upon the level of warning. Exceptionally, where a case borders on gross misconduct and cannot reasonably be disregarded, it is possible to issue a final written warning which will never be removed.

Rules

The ACAS Code recommends that employers set out rules, if possible, in conjunction with the trade unions. Their main function is to specify the types of issues which are regarded by the organisation as potential disciplinary offences and how seriously infringements will be viewed. Reliance upon the existence of rules requires the following conditions to be met:

- Rules must be communicated.
- Special rules must be emphasised and publicised.
- Rules must be specific.
- Rules must be operationally necessary.

Rules must be communicated direct to the individual either in the contract of employment or in separate documentation such as a conditions of service handbook which must be available for consultation by the employee. The ACAS Code recommends that employees are issued with a copy of the rules and that these are explained orally, for example at induction.

Where the employer legislates that certain forms of conduct will result in dismissal, misuse of a free travel pass for instance, this must be emphasised and publicised. It is insufficient to rely upon informal communication or trade union channels. The employer must be able to demonstrate that there could be absolutely no doubt of the potential consequences of violation.

The third requirement, 'rules must be specific', means that if we say theft we mean theft, not unauthorised removal. It is, therefore, essential that rules are sufficiently comprehensive to cover actions associated with theft such as unauthorised usage or appropriation of organisational property or property belonging to another employee. Similarly, if failure to observe financial procedures or regulations will be regarded as a dismissible offence, these should be listed individually.

The mere fact that a particular offence is not listed within the rule book does not, however, preclude the possibility of disciplinary action. Tribunals accept that common sense must prevail and that employees should know that fighting or taking drugs at work, for example, will be viewed seriously.

Edicts which have fallen into disuse must be re-publicised and re-emphasised before being enforced. If, for instance, an instruction forbidding removal of scrap from site has lapsed, it would be unfair to discipline someone for taking material if by custom and practice, others have been allowed to do so. Instead, it should be stressed that henceforth, the rule will be enforced. The penalties for violation should also be made clear.

Rules must be necessary within the context of the business. For example, a social services organisation may forbid certain types of informal contact with clients in order to protect the integrity of the service. Similarly, an employer may insist upon standards of dress or appearance consistent with the image the organisation is seeking to promote. Provided this condition is satisfied, tribunals give employers wide discretion to set standards of conduct. One employer may, therefore, specify dismissal for an offence which another would respond to with a first warning. Provided the rule in the case of the former is operationally necessary and properly publicised, dismissal will be fair, even if it seems harsh.

The phrasing of rules should be consistent with natural justice. That is, it should never be said that a particular infringement *will* lead to a particular sanction, only that it *may*. Similarly, penalties such as 'instant dismissal' are arcane and should not be used as they imply that an employee will be deprived of the opportunity to state his case.

Discipline must be administered consistently. The level of disciplinary action for various categories of offences should, therefore, vary only to take into account the circumstances of each case. Indeed, rarely are two cases identical. Factors differentiating cases include:

- length of service;
- previous record;
- the employee's position within the organisation; and
- the spirit in which misconduct is committed.

Generally speaking, employees with long service should be treated a degree more leniently for the same offence than someone with substantially less service. Conversely, an employee who commits misconduct within a short time of joining the organisation may be treated relatively severely or even dismissed if his employer's trust is destroyed. Similarly, a good record may justify the imposition of a lesser penalty and *vice versa*.

Higher standards may be expected from employees in positions of trust and responsibility. Mis-booking of work by a supervisor, for instance, is more serious than if the offence were committed by an employee because of the latter's position of trust and duty to set an example.

The spirit in which misconduct is committed is also important. Disclosure of confidential information for gain or through malice, for instance, is more reprehensible than a breach of confidentiality resulting from thoughtless tittle-tattle. Likewise, violation of health and safety regulations or damage to property are more serious if done wilfully than if they are the result of a momentary lapse of concentration.

Group dismissals

Where an employer knows that an offence must have been committed by one of a small group but despite reasonable investigation, is unable to identify a culprit, dismissal of the whole group is fair provided the following five conditions are met[†]:

1. That an act had been committed which if committed by an individual would justify dismissal.
2. That the employer had made a reasonable — a sufficiently thorough — investigation into the matter and with appropriate procedures.
3. That as a result of the investigation the employer reasonably believed that more than one person could have committed the act.

[†] In *Parr* v *Whitbread plc t/a Threshers Wine Merchants* Industrial Relations Law Reports, 19 (2) 1990.

4. That the employer acted reasonably in identifying the group of employees who could have committed the act and that each member of the group was individually capable of doing so.

5. That as between the members of the group the employer could not reasonably identify the individual; then provided that the beliefs were held on solid, sensible grounds at the date of dismissal, an employer is entitled to dismiss each member of that group.

Legally, the group can contain any number of employees. In practice, it seems unlikely that the foregoing preconditions will be met if more than three or four are involved.

Appeal pending

It is unnecessary to defer a disciplinary hearing because an appeal against an earlier decision is outstanding. However, reasonable account should be taken of the fact that an appeal is pending in deciding upon a disciplinary penalty.

Multiple involvement

As a rule, where a case involves several employees, investigations should be concluded before anyone is called to a hearing. This depends on the circumstances, however. If, for example, the employer's trust in an employee has been destroyed as a result of gross misconduct, he may proceed at once.

Internal appeals

The ACAS Code urges the provision of an appeals facility and appropriate procedure. ACAS further recommends that employers explain to employees:

- their right to an appeal;
- the procedures for exercising it; and that
- appeals be held promptly.

Grievance procedures are inappropriate for this purpose. A separate right of appeal should be established. Wherever possible, the appeal should be heard by someone senior to the person making the original decision. Likewise, it is desirable that anyone (usually a personnel officer) advising at the original hearing, should not be involved in this capacity at an appeal. Failing an independent appeals body, ACAS suggests that the employee be allowed to reappear before the disciplinary panel to ask them to reconsider their decision.

Natural justice and appeals

The rules of natural justice apply to the conduct of appeals in the same way as they apply to disciplinary proceedings. This implies that:

- *The basis for the original decision must be clear.* In other words, the full case against the employee must be explained to the appeal hearing.

- *The employee must have the opportunity to state his case.* Again, the employee must be afforded an opportunity to explain his side of the case or make a statement in mitigation before the appeals panel delivers its decision. He may also wish to suggest that certain critical evidence or factors mitigating the gravity of the offence were not accorded due weight at the original hearing. Those hearing the appeal must listen patiently and carefully.

- *Those hearing the appeal must be impartial.* Impartiality requires not only an open mind but that proceedings are conducted with scrupulous fairness. Decisions must be reached on the basis of an objective assessment of the evidence and their rationale must be fully explained. Wherever possible, those hearing the case should not have had prior involvement in it.

New evidence

If new evidence is introduced at an appeal it should be considered, and both sides should have the opportunity to comment. New evidence cannot be used, however, to justify a new reason for dismissal or a warning in substitution for the original. In these circumstances, the whole case should be reheard. A decision resulting from new evidence will, thereafter, be fair. However, if new evidence invalidates the original reason for sanctions or dismissal, these should be lifted.

Decisions open to an appeals panel

It would be unfair to impose a more serious sanction at appeal than that decided upon by the original disciplinary hearing. The four options open to an appeals panel, therefore, are to:

1. Remit the case for a fresh disciplinary hearing.
2. Reduce dismissal to a final warning.
3. Reduce a warning to a less serious level.
4. Lift disciplinary sanctions or dismissal altogether.

The first option is appropriate where new evidence is introduced or if the original hearing was procedurally flawed. Alternatively, an appeal hearing can be converted into a disciplinary hearing to rehear the case. If this is done however, a new independent level of appeal must be provided.

Options 2. and 3. are appropriate where the appeals panel concludes that the initial decision was overly harsh or inconsistent with how previous cases have been dealt with.

The fourth option is applicable where the evidence is clearly inadequate, or where it becomes apparent that the case is not a disciplinary one at all, for instance, where the employee's conduct or behaviour results from illness.

The importance of following procedure

It is emphasised that it is dangerous to rely upon an appeals facility to retrieve mistakes in applying the disciplinary procedure. Although the law is as yet unclear, an employee could, in theory, decline to appeal without it affecting him at an industrial tribunal. Although minor failings during any part of disciplinary proceedings may be overlooked provided the employer can show that he has acted within the spirit and intention of fairness, since the *Polkey* judgement, standards have become extremely rigorous particularly for large and medium-size employers. The conduct of disciplinary proceedings must, therefore, aim to follow correct procedure absolutely. The following chapters describe how this can be achieved in practice.

Small organisations and the law

Tribunals recognise that small organisations seldom possess the administrative resources required to carry out extensive investigations and to convene hearings. Generally speaking therefore, the smaller the organisation the less formality and rigour expected. Employers must nevertheless behave fairly and reasonably by:

- informing the employee of the accusation;

- seeking an explanation; and

- making a reasonable decision on the basis of the facts.

Where, for example, dishonesty is suspected, a small employer would simply need to satisfy himself that discrepancies existed and to check obvious possibilities before confronting the employee. Provided the employee is given a chance to explain, and provided the explanation is duly considered, dismissal may take place there and then.

An employee is entitled to receive the reasons for his dismissal in writing. The ACAS Code contains a useful specimen letter. What matters is that the letter clearly states that the employee:

- has been dismissed;

- the reason for his dismissal; and

- the effective date of termination.

The letter may be very short provided it incorporates all relevant details. For example:

Mr S. Jones
14 Land's Crescent
Hathington

Dear Mr Jones

This confirms you are dismissed from today for threatening to hit a customer.

Yours sincerely

While procedure should be followed where possible, leniency is available to small employers. For example, whereas the reason for dismissal should read 'Failure to account satisfactorily for monies in your care'; in the case of a small employer, 'Cash missing from till', though not strictly accurate will be accepted. Always keep a copy of the letter even if it means writing it out twice.

Summary and checklist

- An employee with at least two years' continuous service is eligible to bring a claim of unfair dismissal to a tribunal.

- The burden of proof rests with the employer to show that he acted reasonably. The process is exacting and appeals on points of law may reach the House of Lords.

- Disciplinary and appeals proceedings must be consistent with the three laws of natural justice. These are that:
  - the employee must know the case against him;
  - the employee must have the opportunity to explain;
  - those hearing the case must be impartial.

- Constructive dismissal occurs where the employer breaks, or intends to break, a fundamental term of an employee's contract of employment.

- An employee should not be treated as having resigned until his intentions are clear.

- The purposes of a disciplinary hearing are to establish whether reasonable grounds exist for a belief in the employee's guilt, and, to decide what penalty, if any, is appropriate.

- Proceedings should be instigated promptly and the employee informed of his rights. He must, however, be in a fit state to respond.

- The status of any meeting should be clear. A disciplinary hearing is separate and distinct from a management interview.

- The employee should be allowed a trade union representative or colleague to accompany him to a disciplinary hearing. Such a person may stand surrogate for the employee. If the employee has communication difficulties, an interpreter should be admitted. Legal representation may be disallowed.

- Group dismissals are permissible but subject to stringent conditions.

- The employer must carry out a thorough investigation. This includes examining evidence which mitigates or contradicts his case.

- A hearing must be conducted, no matter how serious the offence or where the employee admits his guilt.

- The employee must have the opportunity to present his case personally to the hearing.

- An employee who fails to attend a hearing may be dismissed *in absentia*, provided he knows that this is a possible outcome.

- Discipline must be administered consistently, and must take into account the circumstances of each case.

- Employers must act fairly in issuing warnings as these lead to dismissal.

- Rules must be communicated, specific, necessary and current. Special rules must be emphasised and publicised.

- New evidence may be introduced at the appeal stage. It cannot be used to substantiate a new reason for dismissal but it is permissible to hear a case again.

- It is unfair for an appeal hearing to impose a more severe penalty.

- The fact that an appeal is pending need not preclude disciplinary action, provided that this is taken into account.

- An employee may decline to appeal without damaging his case at an industrial tribunal.

- Provided an employer can show he has acted within the spirit and intention of fairness, minor procedural errors may be overlooked. However, standards are rigorous and it is dangerous to take risks.

Chapter Two
Dishonesty

Legal principles

The law requires that the relationship between employer and employee must be one of mutual trust and confidence. Consequently, any act of dishonesty on the employee's part will jeopardise this relationship. It is not the magnitude of the dishonesty that is important; the theft or misappropriation of a trivial sum of money for instance may be sufficient to destroy trust and, therefore, leave the employer with no alternative but to sack the employee. This is why most organisational rule books specify dismissal for dishonesty.

In practice, however, it is rarely so simple. Although discipline must always be administered consistently this does not mean that dismissal is automatically appropriate or fair in every instance. Cases vary according to:

- the employee's length of service and previous record;
- the value of the goods;
- the nature of the theft; and
- whether rules are clear and well publicised.

The significance of each of these points is discussed later in this chapter. Here it is sufficient to note that each case must be considered on its merits.

Investigating dishonesty

Involving the police

Where dishonesty is suspected, a prompt and thorough management investigation is essential. Often managers believe their sole responsibility is to telephone the police who will carry out the distasteful task on their behalf. Such abdication is unwise for several reasons:

- It can result in constructive dismissal.

- The police may not wish to pursue the case.

- The police have different interests from management.

- Police involvement may impede a management investigation.

Calling in the police prematurely can result in constructive dismissal because it implies distrust. The pressures upon the police may be such that they are unable to assign priority to the task or pursue it to arrest. The police are interested only in discovering and proving crime. Failure to observe strictly laid down procedures in banking cash for example, are of no interest to them, despite their fundamental disciplinary implications. Furthermore, once the police do become involved, it becomes so much more difficult for management to investigate. They may, for example, sequester records without which management cannot proceed. One such case led to an employee being suspended on full pay for two years pending the return of documentary evidence.

The difference between a police and a management investigation

It is also inadvisable for management to rely upon the outcome of a police prosecution as a court conviction requires a much higher standard of proof than a managerial decision to dismiss.

Essentially a police prosecution requires evidence beyond reasonable doubt, whereas a decision to dismiss requires only a conclusion based on the balance of probabilities following an investigation and disciplinary hearing.

Moreover, criminal proceedings may be dropped because of legal technicalities. It is emphasised that being charged by the police alone does not by any means entitle an employer to dismiss. Dismissal following a court conviction however will normally be fair.

Rights of silence: the difference between police and managerial powers

The police are sometimes called prematurely because it is assumed that they have greater powers to deal with the situation than management. In fact the reverse is often true. This is because an employer has a right to direct an employee to account for his stewardship and is therefore perfectly entitled to require him to answer questions relevant to his employment. The police on the other hand cannot compel anyone to make a statement.

Obviously an employee may decline to answer to management either because he finds it inexpedient to comment or because he has been advised by his solicitor to say nothing for fear of prejudicing himself in court. An employee who elects to remain silent must be told that action will be taken on the basis of available evidence.

Is the employer expected to wait until court proceedings are concluded?

In principle employers are not obliged to await the outcome of court proceedings before acting. In practice, however, due account should be taken of factors such as the date of the court case, whether the employee is a key worker and also his previous record and length of service.

If it is impractical to wait, the best advice is to emphasise to the employee that he is placing his employment in jeopardy by refusing to answer and give him another opportunity to respond. It is irrelevant if the employee is subsequently found not guilty. Provided management have carried out as thorough an investigation as possible and reached a reasonable decision, the dismissal will be upheld.

If the decision is to wait, the employee should be suspended forthwith and informed that a disciplinary hearing will be held as soon as legal proceedings are complete. The latter is essential to ensure that a dismissal is not held unfair because of the delay in holding a disciplinary hearing. At least one representative from the organisation should attend court to hear what is said.

Searching employees

The basic principles are:

- No right exists for employers to stop and search employees unless provided for in the contract of employment.

- Refusal may support a belief in the employee's misconduct.

- Refusal alone is unlikely to validate a belief.

One advantage of involving the police is that they have, or can obtain, powers of search unavailable to management. In certain circumstances it may be necessary to utilise these. It should be remembered however that an employee can always be asked to turn out his pockets, open his car boot, permit access to his garage and so on. Refusal must be considered in the light of all the circumstances, therefore if the employee declines to cooperate, ascertain 'why?' Commonly, the employee will answer that he feels the request is an intrusion on his personal privacy. This can be countered by assuring confidentiality, offering the presence of a woman if appropriate, the facilities of a private office and so on.

Again, guard against acting hastily in conducting a search (whether contractually provided for or not) as this too can lead to constructive dismissal. If a search proves negative be sure to apologise profusely.

Systems failures revealed by acts of dishonesty

Another important reason for holding a management enquiry is that seemingly isolated instances of dishonesty may be symptomatic of profound managerial weakness, a factor of no interest to the police. For instance, an audit enquiry once indicated possible financial misappropriation in a transport depot. Management considered whether to call the police but decided to carry out further enquiries themselves. These revealed such widespread concern among staff about the behaviour of the depot manager that it became apparent that finance was but a small part of a much wider concern. Had the police been called first however, it is probable that the serious underlying malaise which was affecting the quality of working life at the depot would never have been identified.

This is not to suggest that the police should never be called. Clearly where complex or serious criminal activity is suspected, it is important the police are involved. However, it is emphasised that a police investigation is no substitute for a management enquiry. Where possible this should be completed before calling the police.

The need for promptness

All investigations must be undertaken promptly before recollections fade. For example, dismissal preceded by a delay of a week in investigating discrepancies from a cash till was held to be unfair as the operator could not be expected to remember individual transactions for so long (*Marely Homecare Ltd* v *Dutton*). This does not necessarily preclude the investigation of offences originating some time ago, provided the employee can reasonably be expected to account for what has happened. Undue delay in investigating after discovery, however, may lead to unfairness.

Problems in investigating and dealing with dishonesty

Where an employee is caught red-handed it is usually possible to prove the offence beyond reasonable doubt. More often however, the evidence is circumstantial and managers and personnel officers are understandably reluctant to dismiss on the balance of probabilities even though they may be legally entitled to do so. Equally trade unions are often unwilling to see their members subjected to disciplinary action without absolute proof, even if an industrial tribunal does not require it.

Sometimes the amount of money or property is trivial. It may be necessary to balance the seeming harshness of dismissal for a single lapse against the possibility that many more offences might have been committed and the dangers of creating a precedent. The following cases focus upon these difficulties in order to provide a framework for guidance. They also show that dishonesty arises where management create conditions conducive to workplace crime. The chapter therefore concludes with a discussion on security.

Theft: establishing the balance of probabilities

The importance of investigating

Instances where employees are caught in the act of stealing cash or property are relatively easy to deal with. It is vital, however, that even where the evidence appears incontrovertible, management follow proper procedure by investigating and holding a disciplinary hearing because the employee must always be given the opportunity:

- to explain; and

- to say anything in mitigation.

There is always the possibility of an innocent explanation despite appearances. Moreover, the employee must always be allowed to offer a statement in mitigation. Depriving him of the opportunity for either of the above points will render a dismissal unfair. Furthermore, as mentioned earlier, the discovery may herald underlying weaknesses in the organisation's systems or there may be widespread misconduct and malpractice afoot. The case study below is a good example:

A clerk responsible for banking school funds and dinner monies had, over a period of four months, stolen approximately £100 per week, that is one quarter of the takings. The loss was discovered as a result of a routine audit. When challenged, the clerk immediately admitted that she had taken the money. She explained that she was in severe financial difficulties since becoming estranged from her husband who provided her with no money. Initially she had borrowed the cash as an emergency measure with every intention of repaying it. Eventually however, she found herself unable to do so, as her domestic situation worsened and successive thefts accumulated.

The clerk also pointed out that she had succeeded in avoiding detection for so long only because the headteacher never checked the money. The headteacher she said, had unwittingly made it easy for her.

Here the investigation revealed both mitigating circumstances and a serious supervisory failure by the headteacher who subsequently received a written warning. In accordance with correct practice, the plea in mitigation was considered but the offence was judged too serious to be dealt with by a warning. The clerk resigned during the disciplinary hearing.

Is it theft?

In law, theft is defined as the intention to deprive someone of money or property permanently. Consequently, the most usual explanation offered by employees caught stealing is that they were only borrowing whatever they happened to have taken. It may be possible to discredit this claim by thorough and persistent questioning. For example, how long has the employee already been in possession of money or property not belonging to them? By what means do they propose to replace it? Why did they not use their own resources? Unless an employee has been caught selling the goods for example, it is often simpler (and safer) to concentrate upon misappropriation in the case of money, or unauthorised removal where property is concerned rather than call it theft. The key question in both instances is, 'Who gave you permission?'

It should be noted though that whereas organisational rules may specify dismissal as the penalty for theft, they may prescribe a lesser penalty for misappropriation or unauthorised removal. If so, it is necessary either to revert to an accusation of theft if this can be substantiated, or to be prepared to argue the case is sufficiently serious as to warrant dismissal notwithstanding the general guidance contained in the rule book.

Assessing the balance of probabilities

Discovery of workplace crime is often *post hoc*. Dismissal in these circumstances turns on the balance of probabilities, as is illustrated in the case study below.

The takings of a particular canteen cashier were observed to be much lower than those of her colleagues. A system was in operation whereby employees not using the canteen could claim a refund, to the value of 50p, on presentation of an unused voucher.

The cashier was required to 'ring' the transaction in to the till. Examination of the till rolls revealed not only a disproportionate number of refunds relative to other cashiers, (13 to 14 as against 3 or 4), but also a discrepancy averaging £5 a week between the number of refunds 'rung up' and the number of vouchers collected over a period of about a year. When questioned, the cashier said that she was always busy and sometimes forgot to ask for vouchers. She could not account for the disproportionate number of refunds except to say she was always friendly with customers.

Here, there is no proof that the cashier has stolen the money. The questions are: have management carried out a reasonable investigation in the circumstances, and, how might they reasonably respond as a result? Since management have examined and compared till rolls of all cashiers dating back over more than a year and given the cashier an opportunity to account for the discrepancies, the first criterion is partly satisifed. Management must also ascertain whether there is any other possible explanation for the discrepancies. Did anyone else have access to the till for example? In evaluating the cashier's explanation, management need to ask themselves whether such a high and systematic level of forgetfulness is plausible? If the answers to these questions are negative, it seems reasonable to conclude that the cashier has taken the money. Alternatively, disciplinary action could be based on failure to follow the correct procedure in giving refunds, though here the evidence is so strong that it is unnecessary to resort to this approach. As it was, the cashier resigned.

The importance of an open mind when investigating

Having an open mind requires investigators to free themselves from bias and to evaluate evidence critically. Critical evaluation in this context means asking:

- what other explanation might account for the facts; and
- who else has access?

£178 went missing from an office safe over the weekend when the key had been left in the door. The police were called and as a result of their investigations, suspicion focused upon a young clerk who sat next to the safe. The clerk, who was on a low salary, was about to get married. He had a penchant for visiting amusement arcades at lunchtime and was known to be short of money. The police questioned him intensively and indicated to management that they believed he was responsible and that they should pursue the interrogation as they felt he was about to 'break'. Police suspicion intensified when further monies went missing from the safe and the clerk was seen to enter the toilet immediately after the discovery.

As a manager or personnel officer, what are your views so far?

An ex-police officer working in the same organisation learnt of these events and subsequently indicated to management that there were suspicious circumstances concerning the clerk's previous employment in the Civil Service. Enquiries revealed that the clerk had indicated on his application form that his employment there had been temporary. In fact he had been sacked as unsuitable at the end of his probation period. The clerk's explanation was that revelation of this information had cost him several jobs and therefore the Job Centre had advised him to state that his employment was temporary.

How does this information affect your judgement? The clerk (under considerable pressure from management over his falsified application form) resigned. Does this suggest that he was guilty of taking the money also?

That question cannot be answered. What is known is that thefts of money and equipment from the building continued. Eventually one of the caretakers was arrested. Suspicion was directed at him because the thefts always occurred when he was on duty. When police searched his house, they found computer equipment belonging to the organisation and a set of duplicate keys to the building. It also emerged that the caretaker had previously been imprisoned for burglary.

By concentrating their attention on the clerk, management probably missed the real culprit. They allowed themselves to be overly influenced by police suspicions resulting from the latter's own deficient investigation — another reason why management should mount their own enquiries and with an open mind.

Analysing systems failures

The preceding case revealed managerial failures which contributed to the loss. The company's financial regulations required cash to be banked promptly. It should not have been left in the safe over the weekend. Leaving the keys in the safe defeats the object of having one. Furthermore, procedures for handling cash were shown to be inadequate.

During the investigation, another clerk responsible for banking cash and maintaining accounts, admitted of his own volition that on two previous occasions, the money had been £30 short. Believing that he had made a mistake, he made up the deficiencies himself.

Although the clerk's conduct was reprehensible and delayed discovery of a pattern of theft which resulted in the loss of much greater sums, he should not have been solely responsible for handling the money. He would have been much less likely to have committed misconduct if he had been working with someone else. The clerk received a written warning. The loss of the money however was primarily attributable to lax supervision, in failing to maintain basic security and to ensure that financial regulation was properly communicated to and observed by all staff.

Communications failures are at the root of many instances of dishonesty.

Mr Hobson, a porter, was required to report for duty at 7.30 am on New Year's Day. He had no transport and, since there were no buses running at that time, he took a taxi to work. No instructions had been given about transport arrangements but management honoured his claim for the journey to work. They were less happy, however, about his claim for the return journey as this took place at 5.30 pm when a Sunday bus service was in operation. Management were less concerned about the use of a taxi as the receipt for £3.50 had been written on the back of a taxi firm's card.

The informal nature of the receipt attracted suspicion. The taxi firm told management unequivocally that no passenger had been carried that day along the route concerned. Mr Hobson also asserted that he had waited over three quarters of an hour for a bus but none arrived. The bus company however, reported that the service ran to time.

Mr Hobson insisted that he had taken a taxi home and even visited the taxi company and accused them of lying. However, the nature of the receipt and records of the taxi firm and bus company all pointed to a fraudulent claim. Most probably, Mr Hobson (who admitted he had been given a card of the firm who had brought him into work) had attempted to pass it off as a receipt. The handwriting could not be identified as his. Presumably he had asked someone else to write the amount on the card. Mr Hobson's file incidentally, contained an expired warning for mis-booking attendance records and claiming half an hour's pay to which he was not entitled.

The point is that at the disciplinary hearing the trade union official argued that management had been remiss in failing to issue any instructions regarding transport arrangements. While this was primarily a ploy to detract from the real issue, nonetheless it is conceivable that had management said that only inward journeys by taxi would be recompensed, the employee would not have been tempted in the first place. Much unproductive time would therefore have been saved. Mr Hobson received a final warning. Somehow, dismissal seemed a little harsh, partly in view of the amount involved, partly because it was the season of peace and goodwill. Besides, could trust and confidence be broken when there never was any in the first place?

The importance of investigating promptly

Mohamed Jalfrez owed the Council's abattoir £468. The management refused to slaughter any more animals for him until the debt had been paid. Accordingly Jalfrez visited the slaughter house at 8.00 one morning to pay his debt. The offices were closed at that time and notices were posted which clearly stated that all monies must be paid to the cashier. Jalfrez stopped Peter Smith, a slaughterman, and said that he had no intention of waiting till the office opened and insisted that Smith accept the cash. Smith afterwards stated that he put the tightly-rolled wad of banknotes into the pocket of his jeans. When he came to hand the money over however, it was no longer there. Smith could not account for its disappearance. He said that it was probably pushed out of his pocket while struggling to control the animals and either picked up by someone else or washed away in a deluge of blood.

Here management should have stopped everything and mounted a search as soon as the disappearance was reported. What was most likely was that the money was hidden in the building, waiting to be removed once the hue and cry had died down. Obviously it is possible that a search might have revealed unusually high amounts of cash in possession of one or more members of the team. Experience suggests however that no one would have taken the risk. While it might have been possible to retrieve the money, identifying the culprits would have been difficult. Discovery of cash in the building would not necessarily have discredited Smith's story as he might have claimed that someone else had found the money and hidden it. In this case, police involvement would have been helpful as the notes would probably be fingerprinted through contact with blood and other fluids. Even so, the sole existence of Smith's fingerprints on the cash might not prove that he was the only guilty one. The whole team saw Smith accept the money and it was highly unlikely that they would have allowed him to profit from its disappearance alone. Most probably the cash was shared between them.

It is unlikely that police involvement here would have led to claims of constructive dismissal. The suspicion of theft was a reasonable one not least because nearly all of the slaughtermen could boast at least one custodial sentence.

Management gave Smith the benefit of the doubt with regard to theft. They did, however, accuse him of misconduct in accepting the money contrary to regulations and in not taking more care of it. Alas, at the disciplinary hearing, his trade union representative argued that Smith had taken as much care of the money as was practicable in the circumstances. After all, it was not as if he had carelessly thrust it into the top pocket of his overall. Smith, he added, had behaved in the best spirit of courtesy and service towards a client in relieving him of the cash. Management wept.

Dishonesty in obtaining employment

Legal principles

A prospective employee must:

- answer questions truthfully; but

- need not volunteer information.

Unlike insurance, a contract of employment is construed in 'good faith' as distinct from the 'utmost good faith'. This means that whereas in insuring a car for example, there is an obligation to declare everything about the vehicle which might affect the insurer's risk, a prospective employee is only required to answer an employer's questions truthfully. He does not have to divulge information unless the employer specifically asks for it either on the application form or at interview. Therefore, if an employer asks a prospective employee if he has a criminal record, the employee is obliged to answer honestly (unless of course protected by the Rehabilitation of Offenders Act). However, if he is not asked, he is under no obligation to declare it. The caretaker referred to on page 47, for example, could not have been dismissed fairly for having a criminal record as he was not asked about it at any stage of the selection process.

Examples of dishonesty in obtaining employment

Dishonesty varies from wholesale fabrication of biographical details on an application form to subtle evasions, falseness on points of detail, vagueness and exaggeration. Regardless of the magnitude of the offence, the intention is the same, ie to deceive the employer in order to obtain employment or promotion. Those with nothing to lose may commit wholesale falsification which is difficult to detect in the ordinary course of employment interviews as the case below shows.

A man obtained employment within an organisation as a general manager. He was promoted twice and was eventually placed in charge of a centre specialising in providing training for young people with severe learning difficulties. The centre was successful and attracted much publicity, as a result of which someone divulged to a local newspaper that the manager had once been sentenced to life imprisonment for raping and battering a seven-year-old girl to death.

The man succeeded in concealing his criminal background by describing himself as self-employed during the ten years he had been in prison. A reference purporting to be from a previous employer was found to have been written by a fellow convict who had obtained access to his firm's headed notepaper. No one was certain whether the reference had been obtained by post or hand delivered by the employee (the latter method making it easier to commit deception), because there was no indication on file of how it had been taken up. The 'referee' could not be questioned because he died on the day the scandal broke.

Dealing with employees who obtain employment dishonestly

Strictly speaking, an employer is entitled to dismiss anyone who has lied in order to obtain employment if trust and confidence have been destroyed. Each case must, however, be investigated and considered on its merits. The purpose of the investigation is to ascertain whether or not the employee, for example, might have misunderstood a question or made a mistake in completing the application form, as is further illustrated by the following case.

A newly-engaged labourer complained to the personnel officer that he had been 'diddled' out of part of his annual leave entitlement. His leave card showed he was entitled to 20 days. The labourer claimed he should receive 25 on account of his previous ten years' service. The personnel officer was perplexed as he could see no reference to any previous employment with the company on the man's application form.

'I didn't put it down,' he said.

'Why not?' asked the personnel officer.

'I got sacked.'

'What for?'

'Stealing.'

The labourer's explanation was that if he had revealed how his previous employment had ended, he would not have got the job, which clearly indicates his intention to deceive. Balanced against that however was the fact that the labourer was genuinely shocked to learn how seriously his conduct was viewed. Indeed, the organisation's rule book (a most comprehensive document) contained nothing about falsifying application forms. More particularly the application form itself did not carry any *caveat* against dishonesty. Moreover it could be argued that 'rogue behaviour' is not unusual in the nomadic construction industry.

Nevertheless, had management so decided, the labourer could have been fairly dismissed. While a warning regarding the consequences of falsification on the application form would have strengthened their case, the absence of one does not destroy it. A major point in management's favour was that the details concerning previous jobs were checked at interview. The labourer could not therefore say that he had been mistaken as to the information supplied.

It is sometimes said in organisations that double standards apply to the treatment of management and of the workforce. Had a member of the managerial staff concealed information in this way he would, without doubt, have undergone the salutary experience of being sacked again. Here, double standards were applied in reverse as no one had the heart to dismiss. Instead the labourer received a final warning which left him in no doubt about the organisation's expectations concerning trust and confidence in its employees.

Fraud and falsification

Every day organisations lose incalculable amounts through fraud. Detection is difficult because fraud depends on concealment for perpetuation, and because the amounts involved are often marginal and do not readily attract attention. Sometimes, however, they are substantial. An engineering firm for example, noticed that when it switched deliveries to day time, the workshops suddenly yielded ten loads of scrap a week as opposed to three. Similarly, when the auditors were called into a polytechnic the telephone bill mysteriously fell by 50 per cent.

Fraud amounts to dishonesty and, therefore, generally warrants dismissal on the grounds that the employer's trust and confidence in the employee have been destroyed. For example:

An applicant accepted a job, which entailed moving home, as a junior manager of an organisation. He subsequently discovered that the company's removal scheme applied only to married staff. He sought an interview with the director of personnel and pointed out that to move house without assistance would cause him severe financial difficulties as the property was jointly owned with his girlfriend. The director of personnel agreed that in the circumstances, he would pay a removal allowance subject to confirmation of joint ownership.

The manager duly produced a copy of a letter from the building society proving joint ownership. The director of personnel then checked with the building society who said there was no joint ownership and denied authorship of the letter.

The manager resigned in the face of almost certain dismissal for deceit. He refused to explain how he had forged the letter. Asked what made him take the unprecedented step of checking the document, the director of personnel replied that it was a sixth sense. So much for the scientific approach to management.

This case, incidentally, demonstrates the importance of establishing and maintaining basic personnel procedures. Had the removal expenses scheme been explained at interview, or issued to the applicant before he resigned his previous post, this unhappy event might never have occurred.

It is not possible, however, to write procedures to cover every permutation of the human imagination:

Mr Choudry, an Asian, was responsible for administering a budget of £10,000 on behalf of a voluntary organisation. Mr Choudry withdrew the money and deposited it in a friend's bank account. When questioned, he said he had removed the money for safekeeping. He said that because he came from a different culture, he was unaware that this would be viewed as reprehensible.

Careful cross-examination would probably destroy Mr Choudry's case:

- Where was the money lodged to begin with?

- Why did he feel it would be unsafe there?

- Where is his friend's account?

- What type of account is it?

- How long has the money been there?

- What reason had he to believe it would be any more safe in his friend's account?

- Where are the documents relating to the account?

- Have any withdrawals been made? If so, who authorised them?

- What has happened to the interest?

Dismissal for failure to carry out procedures

In some cases of suspected fraud or other dishonesty, it may be safer to concentrate upon role obligations where there is evidence that there has been a serious failure to discharge these. For example, when a stores check at a builder's merchants revealed discrepancies between stocks and issues, the head storekeeper was dismissed not for theft or fraud, but for 'inability to account' for a list of items for which he was responsible. Likewise, an accountant suspected of fraud burned the organisation's records. He was dismissed for wilful destruction of the organisation's property.

It should always be remembered that disciplinary procedures are a means to an end. Therefore, while it might have been more satisfying to secure dismissal for fraud, in both instances the risk of an unsuccessful outcome was reduced by basing the allegations upon concrete, indefensible acts of gross misconduct.

Dishonesty in day-to-day employee/management relations

> He said the project was nearly finished. It hasn't even been started.
> Is there anything I can do about his telling lies?

The short answer to this question is 'yes'. Management has a right to expect truthfulness from employees in all aspects of their employment. There is therefore no reason why a manager, having established that an employee has made a false statement such as this, should not take disciplinary action. A warning letter might read:

Dear

When asked about the progress of the design project, you gave me a categorical assurance that the work was in your own words 'virtually finished'. This statement is reflected in the minutes of the management team meeting of 5 July which state, 'It was reported that the design project is nearing completion. Timescale: two weeks'.

I now find that work on this project has barely commenced. I do not accept your statement that there was any misunderstanding between us. There can be no ambiguity between what you meant and what I understood by the words 'nearly finished'. It would be impossible within a timescale of two weeks to complete the work to the required standard. Moreover at no point did you question the accuracy of the minutes of the management team which were issued the day after the meeting.

It is my belief, therefore, that you have attempted to conceal from me the true state of affairs concerning the project by making a statement which you knew to be untrue. It is imperative to me that I am able to rely upon the word of my staff. I regard this as dishonesty and I warn you . . .

Yours sincerely

Interestingly, while incidents like this occur daily in organisations, they seldom result in disciplinary action. It is outside the scope of this book to speculate on the reasons for this. Suffice it to suggest that most experienced managers are skilled in decoding messages from staff:

- 'It's in typing' — 'I've started it'

- 'I believe so' — 'I haven't a clue'

- 'Making progress' — 'I'd forgotten about it'

- 'It's been sent' — 'Hell, I've lost it'

Preventing theft and fraud

There's £2,000 missing from the safe,' said a manager, 'but it's OK, there's an IOU.'

It has been stressed throughout this chapter that prevention is better than cure. This requires security-conscious systems, proper communication and staff training, and regular monitoring by management. Each of these is discussed below.

Designing security-conscious systems and procedures

Administrative systems and working procedures should be specifically designed to prevent theft and fraud. Employees handling cash should be required to work in pairs. Staff should be moved periodically, forbidden from taking work home and required to use all leave. The same principle applies to property belonging to the organisation. Inventories must be maintained and regularly checked. Security consciousness should be inbuilt. Catering establishments, for instance, often forbid employees to bring bags into the premises. The results of spot checks can be spectacular. The cloakroom of a chocolate factory became littered with discarded boxes after word escaped that searches were taking place at the gates.

Effective communication requires unambiguous rules governing use of vans, recording of mileage, submission of expense claims, issue of protective clothing, stocks and so forth. Quite often organisations forbid employees to remove or purchase surplus stock to eliminate any possibility of misunderstanding. Even well-intentioned procedures however may be open to abuse:

> A scheme operated whereby drivers could purchase vans scheduled for disposal at auction at a favourable price. The aim was to encourage them to take care of vehicles. The result, however, was that many vans nearing the end of their service were sent into the workshops for extensive overhauls. These were then acquired at bargain rates by the drivers.

Rules must be explained

Rules alone are insufficient. They must be clearly and proactively communicated to employees. If employees are to be accused of violation, management must be able to demonstrate that the correct procedures are known and understood. Cases which have to rely upon phrases such as 'common sense', or 'everyone should know', will be perceived as weak and may well fail. For example:

A supervisor responsible for the distribution of pay packets took home those belonging to absent operatives instead of returning them to the security guard. This came to light after an employee reported that he had to wait several days for the supervisor to hand over his wages. When he did receive his packet, the amount of money was correct but he was concerned that it had been opened. The supervisor's explanation was that she had forgotten on each occasion to bring the money in and had opened the packet to check that all the money was there.

Although the organisation regarded this as gross misconduct, it seemed inadvisable to dismiss the supervisor in the absence of any rules concerning the administration of pay packets. Instead they resorted to a final warning. There was no appeal.

Proper communication means there should be written evidence of employees having received and understood instruction in procedures for handling cash and property. Induction or training sessions should be recorded on file and a copy given to the employee. There should be regular updates. At any disciplinary hearing, it is then possible for management to say:

Before being assigned to operate as a cashier, Mrs Jones received instruction in procedures which included the issue of refunds. The handout placed in Mrs Jones's file (copy available) states clearly that a voucher must be received before a refund is made. The handout also emphasises that any failure to carry out these procedures will normally result in dismissal. The handout has been signed and dated by Mrs Jones as confirmation that the contents have been explained to her and that she has understood them. Mrs Jones attended a refresher course two months ago.

Rules must be enforced

Proper supervision also requires regular checks by management. The case of the school clerk referred to on page 44 shows how, typically, thefts of money begin by borrowing. Almost invariably, the intention is to repay, though usually in practice the amounts come to exceed the employee's resources or non-discovery eventually convinces the employee that he is safe from detection. Likewise, pilfering flourishes where employees come to believe that no one is concerned about the odd tray of meat, an old video, some rusting metal and so on, until the whole organisation becomes permeated with dishonesty.

Preventing people from obtaining employment dishonestly

It is sometimes said that plausibility is the hallmark of a 'con merchant' which probably explains how recruiters come to be deceived. The examples of people obtaining employment dishonestly, cited earlier in this chapter, underscore the need for care in verifying the credentials of prospective employees. This applies not only to criminal records but to qualifications, previous employment, reasons for leaving, salary and health record and so forth. Periods of self-employment or unemployment or time spent working for firms no longer trading however, should be scrutinised with particular care though it is appreciated that recruiters seldom have time to check all information. At the very least however, the details contained on the application forms should be confirmed by the employee at interview and recruiters should ask whatever questions they judge apposite. This is to prevent an employee from subsequently claiming that he made a mistake on completing the application form. It is therefore advisable to record on the form itself that the details have been verified. For example:

A new employee's sickness record was giving cause for serious concern. Her application form indicated that she had had 15 days off sick in the last year in her previous organisation which was a branch of the same company. In fact her absence totalled 25 days. When questioned, the employee denied attempting to deceive her employer, saying she had made a mistake when completing the form.

As the explanation was just plausible, and as the sickness record was not checked at interview, no basis for disciplinary action existed.

It is also advisable, especially when interviewing managerial and professional staff, to explore carefully claims as to past experience. Phrases such as 'responsible for all staff', need to be quantified in order to prevent the applicant overselling, or for that matter underselling himself. Similarly applicants' past achievements such as 'introduced new office system' can mean anything from the purchase and installation of a mainframe computer, to issuing an instruction to recycle old envelopes.

Where an employee is suspected of dishonesty it is always a good idea to examine his application form as dishonesty in one arena is often repeated in another.

My first dismissal case concerned an ex-public school boy who, in less than two months, pilfered the petty cash, was granted days off to attend interviews for jobs subsequently found to be non-existent, spent work time in bars and billiard halls and succeeded in losing a receipt book. Having dispensed with his services on grounds of having no confidence, 18 months later I received a request for a reference for him for a job as a policeman. I was asked to confirm that he had worked for us for two years which surprised me. The reply was short and factual stating the correct dates of his employment adding that he was dismissed for a number of offences including dishonesty and that he had the right of appeal but chose not to exercise it. The Inspector telephoned to thank me for the information. The following conversation ensued:

Author:	Did he say he'd been sacked?
Inspector:	No.
Author:	Does he mention that he then worked in a casino?
Inspector:	The cheeky sod.

The applicant was rejected.

Summary and checklist

- Dishonesty often results in dismissal because it destroys the employer's trust in the employee.

- All allegations of dishonesty must be investigated promptly, preferably *before* calling the police.

- A police investigation should never take the place of a management enquiry.

- Calling in the police prematurely can result in constructive dismissal.

- Management has a right to call an employee to account for his stewardship.

- No right of stop and search exists unless provided for in the employee's contract.

- An employee can always be asked to submit to a search.

- Refusal to be searched may be taken into account but refusal alone is unlikely to justify dismissal.

- If an employee refuses to respond to enquiries, he must be told that a decision will be taken on the basis of available evidence.

- Even where the evidence appears incontrovertible, the employee must always have the opportunity to be heard.

- Investigators must keep an open mind,
  - could there be another explanation?;
  - who else has access?

- Usually there is no obligation for management to await the outcome of a court decision.

- Proof of dishonesty is not required, action may be based on the balance of probabilities.

- It is irrelevant if an employee is subsequently found not guilty by a court.

- Where theft cannot be substantiated, dismissal may be admissable for unauthorised removal.

- Dismissal may also be admissable for failure to carry out procedures, provided these are clearly communicated and regularly enforced.

- Dishonesty is facilitated where security consciousness is low.

- Systems and procedures should be designed to prevent fraud and theft.

- A prospective employee must answer questions truthfully, but, he is not obliged to volunteer information.

- Recruiters should take care to verify information on application forms and record responses to questions.

Chapter Three
Performance and Capability

Introduction

The purpose of this chapter is to outline a framework for dealing with problems of poor performance. Specific applications are discussed in the next chapter.

The legal background

The law expects that if an employee professes to possess a particular skill, he is able to demonstrate it in practice. Furthermore, a fundamental obligation of an employee is to exercise reasonable skill and care in going about his work. Dismissal for poor performance may, therefore, either be because:

- the employee is incapable of performing his duties; or

- although the employee possesses the requisite skills and abilities, fails to exercise them.

Incapability is defined as a situation where no amount of training, exhortation or encouragement will make any difference to an employee's performance as he is unable to perform his role either because of incompetence or ill health. Dismissal is therefore normally appropriate as warnings cannot achieve anything. It should be noted however, that ill health dismissals are not disciplinary matters and are, therefore, pursued in a different form to incompetence. The different approaches are described in the next chapter.

Failure to exercise skill and care may be defined as any instance where the employee, though capable, falls short of the requisite standard of performance. This is regarded in law as misconduct as the employee possesses the necessary abilities but fails to utilise them. Normally warnings (formal and informal) are appropriate in order to encourage the employee to improve. Only if the employee fails to respond does dismissal result. Employers have a duty to ensure that employees receive reasonable training and support to equip them to perform acceptably. Sanctions should therefore be preceded by, or combined with, guidance and training.

Practical problems in dealing with performance

Despite the clear legal position, performance is commonly regarded as the most problematic aspect of workplace discipline. A number of reasons may be suggested for this. Performance is often an emotive issue concerning as it does, a particularly sensitive aspect of the employer/ employee relationship. Few poor performers are unequivocally and consistently inadequate. Lapses may occur sporadically or may seem too trivial to warrant disciplinary action. Yet taken together, they erode confidence in the employee. Extraneous factors such as staff shortages and technical problems may make it difficult to apportion responsibility. Similarly, reliance upon team work may obscure individual contributions. At professional and managerial levels, rapid organisational change may lead to frequent variations of job requirements making it difficult to define an employee's role precisely.

The importance of managing performance

Many problems attributed to employee performance actually reflect poor management. Communication is a critical determinant of managerial effectiveness. No one can perform properly without first understanding what is required. Despite this, it is far from unusual to find employees who are uncertain about what they should be doing or how their performance is viewed. Instructions may be carried out without the person properly understanding what is required. Directives may be ambiguous, ill-conceived or ill-thought out, to which the note I once received from my manager bears witness:

> Harold [the director] has got what he wants but he says it isn't what he wants. I don't think he knows what he wants. Please see if you can find out what he wants.

Employee involvement and motivation are also extremely important in promoting performance. Boredom, frustration and alienation may lead to lowered output, decreased attention to quality and so forth. Consequently it is important to stimulate interest, and, if possible, to make work exciting or, at the very least, to ensure that employees understand the importance of their contribution. It is acknowledged, however, that an employee's performance may be unsatisfactory despite these endeavours. Failure to intervene effectively damages:

- organisational effectiveness;

- morale; and

- personal credibility.

The first of these is obvious and requires little comment other than to stress that the opportunity costs of an ineffective employee may be out of all proportion to his rank. A rude or uninterested receptionist for example, may discourage a potential customer from pursuing enquiries. Indeed, in dealing with, say, an estate agency or garage, how often has your custom been lost as a consequence of the behaviour of the office junior?

Morale is seldom enhanced where someone fails to contribute equitably. Organisational effectiveness may suffer if other staff become overworked, embarrassed or angered by a poor performer. Unchecked deviancy may become the norm and lead to a widespread reduction in standards. The damage may be particularly far-reaching if the employee concerned is responsible for staff whose efficacy and job satisfaction are depressed as a result of their superior's performance. They may feel undervalued, even ridiculed through being identified with him.

As manager, you are responsible for the performance of your staff. Their mistakes are your mistakes. Consequently, if you fail to intervene, eventually your own credibility will be questioned. Furthermore your own effectiveness will be reduced if you have to devote time to complete tasks which are someone else's responsibility. In short, you have a duty to take corrective action where warranted. Otherwise, you too are guilty of misconduct.

A strategy and framework for approaching poor performance

The need for a strategy

Although the law expects employers to specify an employee's role and standards of performance, it is accepted that comprehensiveness is impossible to achieve. It is therefore possible (and frequently legitimate) to argue that an employee ought to have known he was required to carry out certain tasks, to certain standards, within certain timescales.

The most robust approach to applying disciplinary measures, however, is to be able to demonstrate that the employee knew exactly what was required of him and thereby exclude argument. This requires a structured approach where all extraneous factors are eliminated step by step. The aim is to exclude all possible excuses such as staff shortages or inadequate training so that the only variable left in the equation is the employee's own performance.

To apply this strategy you need to:

1. Identify the employee's responsibilities.
2. Clarify the required standard of performance.
3. Specify deficiencies precisely.
4. Establish the reasons for the deficiencies.
5. Decide what needs to be done to remedy the situation.
6. Agree an action plan with the employee and set timescales.
7. Arrange a date to review progress with the employee.
8. Confirm the above points in writing to the employee.
9. Hold the progress meeting.
10. Decide what further action (if any) is required.

The steps to be followed are the same for all types of jobs. The first three items are preparatory, aimed at identifying the problem. Precision and objectivity are essential, therefore it is advisable to write down your analysis. This serves as a useful source of reference in discussion with the employee later but more particularly, it is a means of clarifying the issues. If after applying the first three steps you are unable to elucidate your concerns tangibly, then it is unlikely that the problem really is one of poor performance. Each of these steps is now explained in detail.

Identifying the employee's role and responsibilities

First it is necessary to define the employee's role. For many jobs, this is simple. The functions of blue collar workers, craftsmen and basic grade clerical staff, for example, are usually easy to specify and leave little to interpretation. Even less tangible descriptors such as 'Leave in a workmanlike manner' have clearly understood meaning in the context of a particular trade or occupation.

Job descriptions are a useful source of information. It is dangerous to assume, however, that an employee knows or ought to know what is required of him simply because a particular responsibility is encapsulated in his job description. Job descriptions go out of date; they may lack detail or be poorly worded, as this case shows:

An internal audit revealed a finance clerk had passed a number of car mileage claims for which there was no authority. At the disciplinary hearing, management said it was in her job description to authorise claims. The trade union representative replied that she had not seen her job description since she was interviewed for the post, 18 months ago. The clerk had merely been issued with a rubber stamp and told to use it to pass forms for payment. She understood her role was to check the addition. No one had instructed her to verify the claims.

Management then asserted that in any case, the clerk 'ought to have known' that her role entailed more than merely checking arithmetic. Her trade union representative, however, pointed out that the car mileage regulations were contained in a manual which the clerk had never seen, far less had explained to her. There was not even a copy in the office. How then ought she to have known?

This case illustrates the importance of first ensuring that the employee understands what is required of him. Here, management should have ascertained why the clerk had not verified the claims, explained her responsibilities to her and arranged for her to receive necessary information and training. Had she then failed to perform adequately, disciplinary action would be justified. It is stressed that disciplinary action is not precluded by the fact that job descriptions are non-existent or inadequate, provided it can be shown that the employee understands what is required of him. If there is no doubt, however, then the first step in intervention is to specify the employee's role.

Identifying the required standard of performance

Having ascertained what an employee is required to do, the next step is to clarify the required level of performance. It is management's responsibility to set standards. Faced with a problem of poor performance, you must therefore ask yourself, 'What did I expect?' A canteen assistant, for example, may be required to clear tables in a certain manner; a refuse collector may be expected to move bins without causing spillage; a craftsman may need to reach certain output targets. Standards must be defined for all job levels. A common misconception is that expectancies are impossible to specify at senior levels because roles are inherently vague and performance impossible to measure. This is nonsense. A surveyor, for example, may be required to estimate quantities within a given degree of accuracy; a manager may be required to ensure a new computer system is installed and working by a certain date; a director may be responsible for attaining certain profit levels.

Comparisons with other employees are a useful, but by no means the only, way of justifying requirements. VDU operators may average certain levels of output and accuracy. Results achieved by other sales staff may prove that targets are attainable. Where comparisons are unavailable, it is your responsibility as manager to prescribe and defend your requirements. Essentially, defensible standards are those which are attainable on a day-to-day basis, taking into account the employee's professed skills, time allowed for completion, availability of equipment and so forth. Feats of achievement are outside this definition.

Identifying deficiencies in performance

Having established the requisite standards, it is then necessary to measure the discrepancy between these and the employee's actual performance. This may be straightforward. A factory operative, for instance, may have omitted to seal boxes properly and the deficiency is self-evident. Likewise, a lorry driver may have failed to complete delivery notes. More complex cases merit systematic analysis as shown in Table 3.1 below. In the first column, the relevant responsibilities are set out.

Table 3.1: A framework for analysing performance problems

Post	Responsibilities	Required standard	Deficiencies
Receptionist	Answer telephone	Promptness	Callers left hanging on
	Promote good image of organisation	Courtesy	Background conversation
Supervisor	Staff management	Fast and consistent enforcement of rules	Operatives leaving early
	Cost control	Jobs to be completed within budget	Excessive overtime being worked
Manager	Install computerised costing system	Required to plan and ensure that implementation is achieved within agreed timescales	Failure to consult with trade unions has delayed implementation

The required standard is indicated in the second column, and, in the third, the deficiencies are defined.

The role of the receptionist is to answer the telephone and promote a good image of the organisation. The manager then specifies the standards required. These are promptness and courtesy. The problems are that callers are left hanging on and there is a great deal of audible background conversation.

Although the roles become more complex as we move down the table, the method of analysis is the same. Part of the supervisor's role in managing staff is to ensure adherence to rules, yet operatives are leaving work early. The supervisor is expected to control overtime by restricting authorisation to emergencies, yet excess hours are being worked.

In the third example, one of the tasks of the manager is to install a new computerised costing system within a given timescale. This requires him to consult formally with the trade unions as part of a general responsibility for actively promoting employee relations. His failure to do so has resulted in a dispute which has halted the programme.

Evidence is required to substantiate concerns. In addressing the problem of the receptionists, for example, the manager should make a few calls to experience the response first hand. He should note to whom he spoke; the date and time (was it a peak period for instance?); the response; length of time taken to process the call; and details of any background conversations. In the second example, the supervisor is failing to control overtime properly. Precision, however, requires the manager to identify his expectations. For example, he might expect the supervisor to make decisions on what is an emergency, to give permission for overtime to be worked and to inspect work. Expectations can then be translated into questions. In the third example, the manager, for instance, might be asked:

- How many meetings were held with the trade unions?

- Was an agenda circulated beforehand?

- What was discussed?

- Were minutes produced?

- Who was responsible for acting on decisions?

- What action has been taken?

In short, what evidence is there that the manager has exercised initiative in ensuring proper consultation with the trade unions?

Diagnosing the problem and obtaining improvement

By following this process so far, you are now clear:

- what the employee's role is;
- the standards you expect; and
- what is wrong with the employee's performance.

The next stage is to interview the employee to explore the reasons for the deficiencies and to decide together what needs to be done to remedy matters. This is a potentially emotive encounter. There are 12 key steps to effectiveness.

1. *Be prepared*
Have in front of you all the information concerning the problem. Prepare a list of questions. Re-read everything shortly before the interview to ensure you have grasped the details.

2. *Explain the purpose of the interview*
Tell the employee how you intend to conduct the meeting. For example, you may wish to describe the general problem first and then go through each concern in detail. Stress that the employee will be invited to comment.

3. *Avoid making personal attacks*
These will only raise the temperature and make the employee defensive. Refrain from accusations such as 'Your telephone manner is appalling'. Instead, use a problem-solving approach. Open, for example, with, 'I need to discuss a problem with you about answering the telephone'. Keep emphasising 'the problem'.

4. *Be specific*
Tell the employee exactly what is wrong. Avoid circumlocution such as 'Er, um I have now for some time been concerned about the er, um, level of overall productivity within the garage and er well not yours in particular I do hasten to add. You mustn't think I'm being critical...' Just say 'I was wondering why you didn't manage to get through your quota of repairs?' Defining the problem is critical as it forms the basis of all subsequent actions.

5. *Substantiate your concerns with evidence*
Show the employee or describe to him examples of your concerns. This is important because it compels the employee to acknowledge reality and obviates the excuse that he is the subject of innuendo or victimisation.

6. *Listen actively to the employee's response*

This requires an open mind and sensitivity to the tone and emotional content of what is said. It is very easy to shut out information either because it seems to have been said before or because it is assumed that the employee is merely making excuses when he may actually be saying something significant. This applies with particular force where the employee's response is critical of management, including your own performance. Censure is discomforting but it is important to evaluate it objectively and reply. If it is valid then it must be acted upon. If it is not then it must be rejected. Either way, the aim is the same, that is to eliminate it as a possible excuse for the employee's failings.

Furthermore, it is important to be alert to subtle nuances of speech as these may herald a change in attitude or the existence of personal problems. For example, the employee may be signalling that he has now accepted his performance is inadequate and, that he is incapable of meeting requirements.

7. *Keep the discussion to the point*

Anger and distraction are common evasion tactics. Emotion is a spiral and therefore the best way to handle someone who is angry is to wait until the aggression subsides, if necessary by getting him to repeat himself. Distractions usually involve focusing upon trivial or irrelevant points, countered by interjecting with 'That's not the point . . .' and returning firmly to the issue. Politeness is sometimes interpreted as weakness and therefore it may be necessary to combine courtesy with forcefulness. Always maintain your temper. If you do become angry, adjourn the interview and tell the employee why. If the employee becomes tearful, allow him to compose himself but make it clear that the interview will continue. Rarely will it help if you start crying too.

8. *Probe*

Diagnosis requires a thorough exploration of all the symptoms. Through questioning, you may become aware that failure to attain targets for instance results from ineffective delegation. Only by identifying the underlying causes is it possible to effect improvement. For example, a trade union official complained that a personnel assistant had behaved provocatively in saying 'Besides [*sic*] you can't take us to a tribunal, the case is out of time'. When questioned, the personnel assistant said that he had been trying to be helpful by reminding the official that the time limit for pursuing an appeal at an industrial tribunal had expired. Probing it revealed that the real problem was the personnel assistant's poor self-awareness as he was completely insensitive to how he had been perceived.

Other underlying reasons for poor performance may be a failure to plan, failure to prioritise work, failure to delegate effectively or to see projects through properly. Poor health or personal difficulties may be a cause and an effect of poor performance. Stress, too, depresses achievement. It is important to note that it can be caused by under-stimulation as well as overload. Probing is also necessary to gauge whether an employee's responses are genuine or whether he is making excuses. Pressure of work, for example can be assessed by saying 'I see. Well, let's build up a picture of what you have been doing lately'. A careful examination and appraisal of all of the employee's activities should then follow.

9. *Summarise*

Recapitulate each of your concerns and the employee's response. This ensures that both parties have understood the discussion and equally important, defines the employee's position in readiness for succeeding stages of the process.

10. *Respond to the employee*

So far, your role has been mainly to listen and to probe. You now need to explain to the employee how you now view matters. If it is appropriate, state whether and how far you accept excuses or denials. For example you might say:

> You said you were unaware that it was your responsibility to monitor overtime and that it is not included in your job description. I accept it is not mentioned in your job description but I fail to see how you can have been unaware of your role as the minutes of the last three staff meetings which you attended make unambiguous reference to the need for supervisors to control overtime.

11. *Obtain a commitment to improvement*

Discuss with the employee what must be done, by whom, when and how. The receptionist for example, may be required to follow a procedure in answering the telephone and to refrain from personal conversations while operating the switchboard. The supervisor may be required to implement a system of inspection and control. The manager may be instructed to hold regular, formally minuted meetings with the trade unions.

Lowering expectations for a time may help restore an employee's confidence. Sales targets may be reduced; a teacher may be relieved of certain classes; the deadline for completion of a project may be relaxed. Where an employee has suffered major trauma or illness, return to work may be facilitated by starting at the most basic level and allowing him to discover his own level of competence. For example, a secretary/PA might begin with clerical duties, progressing to more complex tasks until he is either eased back into his old job or finds his new level of capability.

Although you must retain the initiative, it is important that the plan is agreed with the employee both to create commitment, and as evidence that you have acted reasonably. If the employee is unwilling to cooperate, ask the reason. Be prepared to exercise some flexibility over targets and timescales but remain resolute over principles. If the employee is intractable, point out that your requirements are reasonable and mandatory.

Hostility and over-reaction can be reduced, even avoided, by maintaining a sense of perspective. Emphasise that provided the requisite improvement is attained, the problem will be resolved. Create a positive note by acknowledging the employee's strengths and contribution.

12. Confirm the interview in writing

Unless this is done, the previous 11 steps will be redundant. Written documentation serves both as an *aide-mémoire* and, equally important, as proof of a reasonable attempt to resolve the problem informally. File notes or cryptic references in a diary will not do. A detailed letter or memorandum is required, set out in accordance with the following checklist.

Checklist for confirming a performance interview

1. The date and place of the interview.
2. The reason for the discussion.
3. All the concerns discussed.
4. The employee's response.
5. Your response to the employee, including your diagnosis of the problem.
6. Positive aspects of the employee's performance.
7. The action required and review date.
8. Any training or assistance offered.
9. Consequences of failure to meet standards.
10. A general offer of support.

This example of a confirmatory letter shows how these points can be incorporated.

①→ Thank you for coming to see me on Tuesday.

②→ I asked to see you to discuss a complaint from Mr Steward, the Headteacher, concerning an altercation between yourself and him on Monday when he entered the school kitchen to ascertain why the lunch was late.

③ → I explained that Mr Steward had two concerns. First, it was the third time in a month that lunch had been late and afternoon classes disrupted as a result. Second, he felt you were rude and abrupt towards him.

④ → You confirmed that the meals had been late and said it was because of the recent cut in staffing. You said Mr Steward was aggressive and that 'You were only defending yourself'.

⑤ → I too am concerned about meals being late. An important part of your role as supervisor is to ensure that lunch is always ready on time. I do not accept your point that you are short staffed. Your kitchen has the same number of employees as other comparable establishments.

Mr Steward admits he was angry. This was because a bus had been hired to take the children out immediately after lunch and he knew they would now be late in setting off. I feel, however, that as supervisor, you could have dealt with the situation more effectively. You should have remained calm in the face of Mr Steward's annoyance instead of becoming angry and defensive. This only made the situation worse and was all the more inappropriate because it took place within earshot of other staff.

I know that you were disappointed after unsuccessfully applying for promotion earlier this year. You said that your motivation has since declined and agreed that as a result, you have devoted insufficient attention to planning which accounts for meals being late sometimes. I note for instance, that you make no use of convenience foods which we agreed would eliminate the problem by reducing preparation time.

⑥ → Mr Steward said that the standard of meals is high, which I endorse. I am confident, therefore, that with a little more experience, you will be eligible for promotion. Given your qualifications and experience, you might have something to offer in the private sector if you are willing to consider this.

⑦ → I now require you to ensure that meals are delivered on time and to improve your interpersonal skills. Please therefore would you revise your menus incorporating convenience foods and discuss these with me next week. I shall then see you at fortnightly intervals for the next two months in order to monitor progress.

⑧ → I will arrange for you to attend a course to assist you in improving your interpersonal skills.

⑨ → Finally, I must reiterate that if your performance fails to improve I may have to take disciplinary action against you. I hope, however, that this will not be necessary.

❿→   You can come and see me whenever you need support or guidance. I look forward to discussing your progress at our next meeting.

Yours sincerely

First, note how the employee's role is made clear. She is responsible for meals being ready on time and for handling complaints. The manager has not allowed himself to be distracted by excuses. Secondly, the consequences of mismanagement are described, showing that the manager had good reason to intervene. Circumlocation such as 'Had a severe impact upon the organisation and management of the schedule of activities', is avoided. Instead, the explanation is clear and simple; because the meal was late the children were late boarding a bus ordered to take them out for the afternoon. Having refuted the supervisor's statement about staff shortages, the manager suggests that lack of planning stemming from depressed motivation is the real cause of the problem. It is noted that both parties agree that the solution requires more use of convenience foods. The manager knows that the supervisor is volatile. Training is offered but he refrains from becoming responsible for teaching interpersonal skills. The reference to alternative employment has been carefully phrased to obviate claims of constructive dismissal. The words '. . . if you are willing to consider', show that it is the employee's decision. They may also have a therapeutic effect of making the employee feel she is in control of her career.

The potential consequences of failure to respond are clear. Elaborate language such as '. . . may have an adverse impact upon your employment' is avoided. The concluding offer of support is further evidence that the manager has done everything that could reasonably be expected of him to support the employee. Overall, the document should convey an impression of reasonableness and thoroughness. When composing it, therefore, imagine how it will sound read out to a hearing or industrial tribunal.

Experience suggests that where performance is dealt with in this manner, the employee, having understood what is required of him and experienced management's resolve, either leaves or improves. Seldom does the need for disciplinary action arise. If it does become necessary to produce the document in a hearing and its accuracy is challenged, counter by asking why this was not mentioned when it was issued. In practice, however, if the letter is comprehensive and incorporates the employee's response (albeit that you clearly disagree with it), seldom will it be questioned. The sooner after the meeting the document is issued, the more likely is an outsider to be persuaded of its accuracy.

Some trade unions object to informal warnings because they perceive them as *de facto* disciplinary action from which there is no appeal. If a protest ensues, ask whether the letter contains anything which was not said at the meeting and make a note of your conversation. Point out that it would be unfair to proceed straight to formal action in view of the need for the employee to understand his role, receive training, discuss problems and so forth. Emphasise that the purpose of the document is to avoid the need for sanctions by alerting the employee to how his performance is viewed. Be prepared to amend any part of the letter which is factually incorrect. Otherwise, if pressed, insist that the issue is non-negotiable. Never under any circumstances agree to withdraw the letter.

Indeed, many trade union officials accept this method of management and may even tell the employee (privately), that he is fortunate not to have been formally disciplined. It was stressed in the introduction to this book that more problems are caused by managers circumnavigating procedures than by those intervening in an objective and systematic manner. Nowhere does this apply more than where poor performance is concerned.

Furthermore, failure to attempt to resolve problems informally will almost certainly be challenged at a disciplinary hearing:

> When did management ever indicate to my member that they were concerned about my member's performance? When did they ever counsel him or give him any feedback? What support or training has my member ever received from management? When have they even taken the trouble to explain to him what his job is?

13. *Review progress*

The employee must be given reasonable time in which to improve his performance. Reasonableness is determined by the nature of the problem and operational exigencies. Obtaining contracts for sales of products with long lead times such as software systems requires a longer timescale than where goods are sold over the counter.

It is essential that the commitment to review progress is enacted, otherwise the whole process is discredited. It is appreciated that time pressures and competing priorities may make it difficult to spend time with the employee and therefore monitoring often lapses. This is counter-productive as it makes it all the more difficult to broach the problem later.

Consequently, it is important that the amount of support offered and the extent of the review period are realistic. As a guide, the more senior the employee, the less attention he can expect. If operational reasons restrict the availability of assistance, or the length of time you can afford for the employee to improve his performance, these should be explained.

It is permissible to intervene before the review period has expired if there is evidence that operations are suffering intolerably or that the situation is hopeless. Acting reasonably does not necessitate jeopardising the organisation.

Satisfactory progress

Where targets have been attained and confidence in the employee is restored, the review should be concluded in writing as follows:

- Confirm that the employee is now performing satisfactorily.

- Remind him that the improvement must be sustained.

- Make a general offer of continued support and assistance.

For example:

> Dear
>
> Further to our meeting on 1 September I am pleased to confirm that your standard of workmanship is now satisfactory. Provided this improvement is maintained, I will not need to see you again. However, as emphasised in our meetings over the last three months, should you experience any problems affecting your performance you can come and see me at any time and I will do my best to help.
>
> Yours sincerely

This note is worded to impress the reader with the amount of attention devoted to the employee and management's goodwill. It shows that the problem is a long-standing one and shows management's patience in seeking to resolve it informally. Moreover, the employee is prevented from subsequently claiming that he was unaware that he could, or should, seek help.

Unsatisfactory progress

Where an employee has failed to improve sufficiently, it is necessary to decide whether to:

- extend the review period; or

- proceed to disciplinary action; or

- seek some other solution.

This in turn will depend upon whether an employee has:

- made partial progress; or

- made no progress; or

- is incapable.

Partial progress may justify an extension of the review period if there is a strong possibility that, given more time, the employee will reach an acceptable standard. Where the employee's response has been negative or seriously inadequate, a formal warning is required. Rarely is it apposite to proceed from counselling straight to dismissal. Unless the employee is incapable, he should be given further chances to improve.

Where an employee is incapable of all or part of his duties, alternatives to dismissal range from changing his job requirements by excusing him from specific duties to a disciplinary transfer. The former generally has little to recommend it because of the likelihood of resentment from other staff. Furthermore, the wisdom of accepting partial performance in return for full pay is doubtful. However, where the allowance is minor (say less than 5 per cent of an employee's duties), or where an equitable exchange of duties can be arranged, the idea may be worth exploring.

Disciplinary demotion or transfer is only an option where an employee's contract specifically provides for it or where the employee consents. There is no obligation in these circumstances to offer an employee alternative work. However, if suitable openings are available, it is reasonable to do so. Suitable means anything which the employee is equipped to undertake. The fact that a transfer might require him to relocate or accept less pay or diminished status, is immaterial, though again, it is reasonable to seek to satisfy an employee's aspirations. Dispel any myths, however, that the employee has a right to so many refusals or to insist upon special terms and conditions.

Equally, never assume that because a transfer entails a lower salary, or is otherwise potentially uncongenial, the employee will decline. Make the offer, be clear about the possible disadvantages but otherwise present it positively. Then, most important, give the employee ample time to consider it. Although his initial reaction may be negative, allowing time to reflect, time to calculate finances and talk matters over, increase the likelihood of acceptance.

Beware of becoming accused of constructive dismissal. While it is permissible to advise an employee that dismissal is a probable outcome of disciplinary proceedings, it should never be regarded as a certainty. Emphasise to the employee that he will have the opportunity to respond to management's concerns at the disciplinary hearing and that the outcome is by no means a foregone conclusion. (See Chapter One for further information.)

Normally, offers of alternative employment are intended to obviate holding a disciplinary hearing. It is permissible, however, to hear the case and then make an offer as an alternative to dismissal.

Combining sanctions with voluntary demotion

This option may appear illogical but it is often attractive to managers and is permissible, provided the employee agrees. The purpose of the warning is to emphasise to the employee the extent to which management's patience has been tried and so pave the way for more serious disciplinary action should the employee's performance continue to be unsatisfactory. If other misconduct has been committed, this too should be addressed as part of the disciplinary process. For example:

A school caretaker was accused of lateness, leaving work without permission, poor performance and falsifying time sheets. He claimed the full hours on days when he had actually been late, or left the premises during the day. He explained that his wife had thrown him out and that he was sleeping on his mother's settee. Discomfort, and marital and financial worries caused him to lie awake and then oversleep. He needed time off during the day to see his solicitor and welfare benefit agencies. He was short of money, therefore had not recorded his absences on his time sheet.

He was aware that his performance was inadequate. His marriage had broken up because he drank heavily as relief from the responsibilities of his job.

Normally, dishonesty alone would have resulted in dismissal. In view of the mitigating circumstances however, management were reluctant to sack him even though they had no confidence in his ability as caretaker. The solution was to combine the offer of an assistant's post with a final warning.

Analysing and diagnosing performance failures

Much has been said about the importance of identifying the underlying causes of performance failures and the value of an analytical approach in achieving this. The following method is a powerful tool which will enable you to:

- gain a firm grasp of the issues, and, form the basis of a sound case if disciplinary action is subsequently necessary;

- deal with the problem authoritatively, thoroughly and factually;

- distinguish symptoms from causes and so yield a penetrating and accurate diagnosis.

A methodology for analysing performance failures

The steps involved are identical for all job levels as follows:

1. Establish the facts.
2. Verify the facts.
3. Analyse the facts to identify every performance failure.
4. Establish what is involved in carrying out the task. How complex is it? Is cooperation from other people or departments required?
5. Obtain an explanation for every failure.
6. Evaluate the reasonableness of the explanation.
7. Assess the implications of findings.

The best way to demonstrate the use of the model and its value is through a worked example as follows:

> An ex-employee wrote to the salaries department to claim holiday pay to which he was entitled. After waiting three weeks for a reply, he telephoned the administrative officer and was told that his claim would be dealt with 'as soon as possible'. A further five weeks elapsed and still the employee had received nothing. He then wrote to the chief accountant. On learning that a complaint had been made, the administrative officer then wrote to the employee stating 'Your claim has now been authorised'.

Ostensibly here is a case of tardiness which might be addressed by apprising the administrative officer of the required timescales and issuing a warning, perhaps informally. However, as the following analysis reveals, such a response would be only partial.

Establishing the facts

A clear grasp of facts is essential to provide a framework for analysis. This should be set out in chronological order so that it is clear what took place, and when. In this case, it is necessary to list the date the claim was lodged, the dates and substance of subsequent telephone calls, the date and contents of the letter of complaint and the subsequent processing of the claim. Listing these not only facilitates checking, but also establishes a picture of what has happened.

Verifying the facts

All information must be confirmed before proceeding. The chief accountant checked the file, contacted the complainant and interviewed the administrative officer in order to satisfy himself that the details contained in the letter of complaint were factually correct and complete.

Analysing the facts to identify performance failures

A good method is to consider each fact in turn and list the concerns arising as follows:

1. *Fact*
   Claim lodged 8 March.
   Concern
   Why was it not processed immediately?

2. *Facts*
   Employee telephoned three weeks later, told claim would be dealt with 'as soon as possible'.
   Concerns
   Why was the claim not dealt with then?
   Why was the employee not given a definite timescale?
   Why was no apology made for the delay?

3. *Facts*
   Employee complained to chief accountant when claim still had not been paid five weeks later.
   Total of eight weeks had now elapsed.
   Concerns
   When would this claim have been paid if not for the letter of complaint?
   How does this reflect upon the organisation?
   Why did the letter to the employee not indicate when he could now expect to receive payment?
   Why did aforesaid letter contain no apology for the delay?

Establishing what is involved in a task

It is important to understand the skills required and the complexities involved in carrying out a task before inviting the employee to explain his performance. The chief accountant ascertained from the administrative officer that processing the claim was a routine operation requiring a two-line memorandum to the payroll section and a brief letter of confirmation to the employee.

Establishing an explanation for every failure

Thus armed, the chief accountant went through his concerns with the administrative officer. Not only did he seek to understand why it had taken over eight weeks for the claim to be processed but also why no apology was ever offered for the delay. The administrative officer first suggested that he was unaware that there was any specific turn-round time for claims. This was refuted, as clearly eight weeks to process a pay entitlement is unacceptable by any standards. Then the administrative officer pleaded pressure of work. This too was rejected as the task was literally a five-minute one. When questioned about his failure to apologise at any stage, the administrative officer admitted that he had been annoyed when the employee telephoned him and had let him wait as a punishment. Asked whether the employee had been rude or aggressive, the administrative officer replied that he had taken exception to being telephoned at all. When the matter was probed further by the chief accountant the administrative officer eventually stated that the fuss was incomprehensible, as in his previous organisation, a public bureaucracy, this standard of service was the norm, as was vindictiveness towards clients regarded as troublesome.

Evaluate the explanation

The chief accountant concluded that there was no reason why the claim could not have been dealt with promptly. Not only was the delay inexcusable but the administrative officer's behaviour towards the employee was unacceptable.

Assessing implications of findings

What appeared at the outset as a simple case of tardiness or forgetfulness clearly reveals a most unsatisfactory attitude towards the job and towards clients. The results of the analysis can then be used to indicate to the employee where his performance is inadequate, and the standards required:

- The claim concerned payment of salary to which the employee was entitled. It should, therefore, have been processed immediately or within two to three days at the most.

- The administrative officer's response after the claim had already been neglected for three weeks that it would be dealt with 'as soon as possible', was unsatisfactory. It showed lack of courtesy and lack of any notion of service to the client. He should have apologised profusely and undertaken to deal with the claim at once.

- Not only did a further five weeks elapse, but, had it not been for the letter of complaint, it was unclear when, if ever, the claim would be dealt with.

- The letter eventually sent to the complainant was completely unsatisfactory. It contained no apology, no explanation for the delay, nor did it even state when he would receive the money.

- The administrative officer allowed his personal feelings to influence his performance. This is unacceptable.

In short, applying this methodology has enabled the chief accountant to identify the real problem which is that the administrative officer's view of what is acceptable falls substantially short of the standards required. Note how the chief accountant opened with a general question about the length of time taken to process the claim before moving onto specific delays. This immediately yielded the answer that the administrative officer was unaware of turn-round times and avoided the accountant's becoming embroiled in a series of excuses which might have occurred, had he tackled each phase of the delay initially. The chief accountant then began to address each concern step by step. Having already established that the task was a simple one, he was immediately able to reject pressure of work as an explanation. This forced the administrative officer to think again and so the real reasons for the delay and discourtesy were revealed.

Summary and checklist

- An employee professing to possess certain skills must be able to demonstrate these in practice.

- The law expects an employee to exercise reasonable skill and care in going about his work.

- Poor performance may result from incapability or misconduct. Warnings are inappropriate where the employee is incapable as they cannot achieve anything.

- An employer has a duty to ensure that an employee receives reasonable support and guidance to equip him to perform adequately.

- Poor performance not only impairs organisational effectiveness, but also your own managerial credibility.

- Extraneous factors frequently obscure individual contributions. A systematic approach to poor performance aimed at eliminating potential causes is, therefore, required.

- An employee must know what his role is and what standard of performance is required. You too must be clear. Ask yourself 'What did I expect?'

- Be factual, direct and specific. Substantiate your concerns with evidence. Never evade the issue or confuse the employee with circumlocution.

- Performance is a potentially emotive topic. Hostility can be reduced by objectivity, taking a problem solving approach and maintaining a sense of perspective.

- Always confirm performance interviews in writing and honour commitments to review progress.

- Pledge only such assistance and support as you can actually deliver. It is permissible to intervene before the end of a review period if necessary.

- Disciplinary demotions or transfers are only permissible if provided for in the employee's contract or if he agrees.

- It is essential to diagnose and address the underlying causes of performance failures. This requires a detailed analysis of the facts, and the ability to identify potential disciplinary implications.

Chapter Four
Dealing with Specific Problems of Employee Performance

Introduction

The purpose of this chapter is to show how the framework outlined in the previous chapter can be applied to various types of performance problems. Incapability is covered first, followed by misconduct. Incapability is defined as inability to carry out the role, functions and responsibilities of a particular job. It results from either:

- incompetence; or

- ill health.

Each of these requires a different approach and therefore is covered separately.

Misconduct is defined as failure to exercise skill and care. Particular attention is paid here to the importance of clear role definition and training. This section also includes advice on dealing with long-standing performance problems and personality clashes. It concludes with a methodology for assessing managerial performance at senior, middle and junior levels.

Incompetence

Strictly speaking, selection procedures should eliminate incompetent applicants. It is appreciated, however, that these procedures are seldom perfect. Incompetents commonly gain entry as a result of recruiters' assumptions about the transferability of skills. Although it is reasonable to assume that someone who has served an apprenticeship or obtained a professional qualification is basically capable, nevertheless it is essential to probe their experience. An electrician, for example, may be used to domestic repairs and prove incapable of the task of wiring an industrial complex from scratch. A salesman, skilled in high pressure techniques, may be unable to adopt the different approach required to sell computer software to senior executives. A highly qualified and experienced hospital nurse may not possess the interpersonal skills needed to work in a health centre. Similarly, employees promoted from technical or professional roles to managerial positions may not be equipped to perform as managers, even though they are technically competent.

The probability of recruiting incompetents increases where appointments have to be made quickly, or where the field of candidates is poor, or both. In these circumstances, recruiters are understandably willing to take risks rather than incur the costs of an unfilled vacancy.

Is the employee incompetent?

The joiner who is unable to saw wood, the machinist who cannot sew a pair of trousers, are manifestly incompetent. Some cases, however, are more problematic.

A company urgently needed engineers to complete contracts. Demand exceeded supply, consequently there were few applicants. A Mr Woo Sang, native of Hong Kong was interviewed. Reservations were expressed about his spoken English as he was unable to respond intelligibly to questions. It was concluded, however, that this probably reflected interview nerves, as his qualifications and written English were excellent. Unfortunately, once in post, Mr Woo Sang was unable to make himself understood, particularly over the telephone where much of his work was conducted.

Is Mr Woo Sang incompetent? Conceivably, with training and encouragement, his spoken English would improve. Employers, however, are not expected to teach employees the principal elements of their role. If someone professes to possess a certain skill, he must be able to demonstrate it in practice. Yet did Mr Woo Sang say he spoke fluent English? No one could be sure, as his answers at interview were incomprehensible. Applying the definition of incapability, however, it can be reasoned:

- fluency in English is a fundamental job requirement; and
- Mr Woo Sang is incapable of it; therefore

- he is incompetent.

Interestingly, although they could have dismissed him, the organisation decided to utilise Mr Woo Sang's excellent technical abilities as best they could while arranging for him to attend English lessons.

Incompetence at senior levels

Incompetence can be particularly difficult to determine at senior levels. The signs are often evident at the outset, but are rarely unequivocal. For example, adverse reactions of colleagues to the newcomer may be the product of jealousy. Similarly, although the employee's behaviour (conduct in meetings for instance) may be unimpressive, time is necessary for the results of his performance to become evident. Understandably, there is a tendency to trust that, eventually, all will be well. This hope rarely materialises. Meanwhile, the damage to the organisation accumulates and the incompetent executive becomes entrenched.

An analytical approach to investigating incompetence

The longer an employee remains in post, the more difficult it becomes to argue that he is incompetent. It is vital, therefore, that indicators of incapability are investigated immediately.

> The first task undertaken by an assistant director of health education was to draft a leaflet on AIDS. The result, produced in biro and illustrated with matchstick men, made him a laughing stock especially as the assistant director complained that it had taken eight hours of his weekend, and that he was exhausted.

Although this account inspires little confidence in the assistant director, can it be concluded that he is incompetent? Analysis reveals:

Facts

- The task was simple.

- The amount of time consumed was inordinate.

- The results were totally unsatisfactory.

- Despite its simplicity, the work has drained him.

- He has taken exception to working at the weekend.

- It was actually inappropriate for an assistant director to carry out the task.

Concerns

- Does the assistant director possess the requisite mental abilities?
- Does he possess sufficient mental stamina?
- Is he committed to the job?
- Is he aware of the need to delegate by directing and coordinating the work of others?
- Is he capable of doing so?

Such a poor result casts doubt over the employee's intellectual ability. The fact that the task taxed him so, suggests his mental stamina is seriously inadequate. His commitment is also questionable. Senior executives must expect to work at weekends. Furthermore, he appears to lack any concept of his role. An assistant director is required to initiate and coordinate specialist input, not to undertake the task himself. However, there is little to suggest he would be able to command the confidence and respect required to manage a bright and articulate inter-disciplinary group.

To summarise, this analysis suggests that the assistant director's scholastic abilities and stamina are inadequate. Moreover, serious doubt exists over his ability to manage collaborative projects. Whereas managerial skills can be acquired, mental capacity cannot.

Disappointing though his performance was, it seemed premature to declare the assistant director incompetent. As time passed, however, the pattern was repeated. Official complaints from his staff described him as 'lazy, arrogant and stupid', saying that he spent his time idling on the telephone. His concentration they said, was extremely limited and he needed to sleep every lunch time. After 18 months, the Unit was still without any clear objectives, and therefore, a management interview was held. The assistant director did not even realise that he was being criticised. The point is that almost all of these concerns were evident from the start. Had the employee's performance in producing the AIDS leaflet been analysed at the time, he might have been declared incompetent much earlier. Interestingly, he was the only applicant for the job.

A framework for evaluating competence

The first submission of a substantial piece of written work such as a business plan, policy paper or a set of revenue estimates is often a reliable indicator of competence at senior levels. Alternatively, it may be necessary to test the employee's competence by devising one or more projects for him. The following questions may be useful in evaluating the results:

- Is the nature and purpose of the submission clear?
- Is it comprehensible?
- Is the argument clear, logical and supported by evidence?
- Is the document well-written and well-presented?
- If tables are included, are these explained in the text?
- Has the subject matter been researched and covered in sufficient detail?
- Are the options clearly identified and critically evaluated?
- Are the conclusions and recommendations apposite, clear and reasoned?
- Overall, has the submission been clearly thought out?
- Is it consistent with the initial brief?

Before discussing the submission with the employee, first check that he was properly briefed. Second, ascertain whether there were extraneous factors which might have affected the quality of the work. The next step is to investigate how the employee has approached the task. The following checklist may form the basis of a management interview.

Checklist for a management interview

- What did you understand was the purpose of this exercise?
- How does this match the initial brief?
- Please explain in detail how the submission was compiled?
- What does this ... (specify) mean?
- Why do you suggest ... (specify)?
- How was the information contained in the report derived?
- How has this information been verified?
- With whom have you consulted?
- Please would you summarise your argument?

- How did you identify the options listed?

- What criteria did you use to evaluate these?

- On what basis did you draw your conclusions?

- How do your recommendations relate to your conclusions?

- What makes you believe the document is adequate?

- Why does it not contain ... (specify)?

Obviously, not all of these questions will be applicable to every situation. The first three and the last two points are universally relevant and the most telling.

Dealing with an incompetent employee

Inability to perform any one of the major tasks attached to the job means *de facto*, that the employee is incompetent. An airline pilot, for example, was once fairly dismissed for landing his plane the wrong way. The airline said that the skill was so fundamental that failure to demonstrate it, even once, equated to incompetence.

The critical questions are:

- do I have confidence in the employee? and

- if not, why not?

If you are unable to trust the employee and can explain why, then you have the basis for a belief in his incompetence. Depending on his employment contract, a new employee may not be entitled to a disciplinary hearing. Nonetheless, it is good practice to behave as though he were: ie the employee should be interviewed and should hear and, if appropriate, be shown the evidence. He should then be given the opportunity to put his case before being dismissed for incapability. Where the employee is entitled to a disciplinary hearing, this should be held. In practice, few employees resist.

Incompetence and training

An employer may elect to train employees in essential skills. It is stressed, however, that a commitment to train, express or implied, must be enacted before declaring an employee incompetent. Dismissal of a probationary teacher, for example, will be unfair unless he has been afforded proper support, such as the facility of a mentor and in-service training. He must also be allowed reasonable time to develop his skills.

Incapability and ill health

Dismissal for incapability is admissible where there is no prospect of an employee's health recovering sufficiently within a reasonable space of time for him to continue in his job.

Ill health dismissals

Dismissal in these circumstances is not a disciplinary matter. It should be approached sympathetically and in close consultation with the employee. Medical advice is essential, and the employee must have the opportunity to comment on the doctor's recommendations. If a diagnosis of incapability is disputed by the employee, an independent opinion must be obtained. It is stressed that dismissal is a managerial decision. Medical advice informs judgement but does not supplant it. Other factors such as operational needs and the employee's views must be taken into account.

No definitive rules exist on how long an employer must wait before dismissing an employee. If medical advice indicates permanent incapability, dismissal may be fair regardless of the duration of absence or whether or not the employee has exhausted his entitlement to sick pay. Conversely, exhaustion of sick pay entitlement does not automatically bring about dismissal. Even where there is every prospect of an employee returning to work, dismissal may be fair, if he is a key worker and his employer is unable to await his return. In these circumstances, dismissal following a week's absence may be upheld.

Alcoholism

Alcoholism is an exception. Employers are restrained from disciplinary action provided the employee is willing to undergo treatment. The reasoning is that dismissal merely passes the problem on to another employer. It is emphasised, incidentally, that specialist treatment is essential. General support and counselling are no substitute, nor should they ever cut across professional judgement.

The relationship between ill health and performance

Although ill health, as distinct from persistent short-term absence, is not a disciplinary matter *per se*, as Figure 4.1 shows, the relationship between ill health and performance is reciprocal and sometimes, therefore, the two are linked.

Poor performance causes stress and consequently ill health. Conversely, ill health depresses performance. Frequently a self-reinforcing cycle

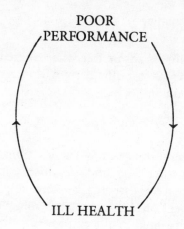

Figure 4.1 The relationship between poor performance and ill health

develops whereby both performance and health deteriorate. The following cases exemplify the importance of determining which factor precedes which in the chain of causality.

> The performance and sickness record of a chief engineer degenerated over a period of about two years. When counselled, he said that he had been lonely and unhappy since his wife was killed in a car crash. Consequently, he was now consuming a bottle of vodka a day.

Analysis reveals three concerns, namely: poor performance; sickness; and deep-seated personal problems. The latter have caused ill health which in turn, has affected performance. In the next case, the causal chain is reversed.

> An accountant used to working in a staid and predictable environment, found himself subjected to pressure and frequently changing priorities in his new job. His initial performance was unimpressive. He explained that he felt stressed over never being allowed to complete one job at a time, and by having his instructions constantly redefined.
>
> He was then off sick for two months with anxiety and depression. When he returned, he did little work, he seemed vague and his eyes were glazed. Every day he would disappear once or twice, sometimes for up to an hour.

Here, incompetence has led to ill health. The employee was redundant when recruited and was selected because there were few applicants. Besides, as he was relatively young (40) it was felt that he could adapt. In fact he was clearly incapable of working under pressure which was a fundamental aspect of his role.

In the first case specialist help and counselling are apposite as the employee is basically competent. They cannot however achieve anything in the case of the accountant. The only solutions are to redeploy or dismiss him as the job is directly causing his ill health.

Employee becomes incapable

Incapability may result from a change in technology or working methods where the employee, through no fault of his own, is unable to adapt or learn new skills. Many organisations have severance schemes for this eventuality. Employers are not obliged to offer these, however, and can either treat the transition as a redundancy situation or deal with the problem on an individual basis by dismissing the employee for incapability if no alternative employment exists. Generally speaking, in these circumstances employers are required to behave reasonably by doing everything possible to help the employee adapt, though without endangering the viability of the organisation.

Incapability can arise in many different ways as this case shows.

> A bricklayer was engaged to work on a building site. For the first fortnight, however, he was deployed repairing garden walls. When he commenced work proper on site, he refused to wear a safety helmet which is compulsory by law. He said it made him ill.

Strangely enough, the employee was told at interview that he would be working on construction sites. Wearing a hard hat was not mentioned because this is something a long-serving bricklayer ought to have known. Medical advice was irrelevant here, though it might be appropriate in the case of a long-serving employee who had suddenly developed a problem. There was no question of the bricklayer's working without a hard hat. It would be reasonable to offer him alternative employment if any was available. Failing that, he should be dismissed for incapability.

Failure to exercise skill and care

The law expects an employee to exercise reasonable skill and care in going about his work. This implies:

- concentration;
- diligence;
- adherence to working methods;
- observance of standards; and
- initiative.

Concentration and diligence mean that a typist, for example, may be expected to work accurately and carefully. He may be required to use a certain system for document retrieval, to achieve reasonable levels of output and deal courteously with enquiries. Initiative means he can be expected to draw authors' attention to errors.

The importance of training

Adequate performance demands adequate training. When mistakes occur, disciplinary action often turns on whether the employee ought to have known, or whether insufficient instruction is to blame. The following checklist may be useful in determining responsibility for failure to exercise skill and care.

Checklist for analysing a performance failure

- Did the employee understand what was required?
- Had he received proper training?
- Did he possess the requisite skills?
- Were equipment and facilities necessary to complete the task available and in good working order?
- Had the employee been properly trained in their use?
- Was the timescale adequate?
- Was supervision adequate?
- Did the employee understand the significance of his role?
- Were there any factors outside the employee's control which might have affected his ability to carry out the task?

- What explanation did he offer for the mistake, and, was it reasonable?

The two following cases illustrate the difference between adequate and inadequate instruction.

> A surveying assistant was instructed to inspect the window frames of every property on a housing estate and count the number of replacements required. This information was then used to tender for the contract. The employee, however, inspected only a small proportion of the windows. Consequently many more frames had to be replaced than had been provided for in the tender price. The result was a £75,000 deficit on the job.

The first two questions on the checklist require affirmative evidence. Here, there was no doubt that the employee understood what was required. Not only did he receive verbal instructions from the group surveyor, but, most tellingly, he was required to place a tick or a cross against the address of every property in order to compute the number of replacements required. Quite different documentation would have been issued for a sample survey. Furthermore, the returns submitted indicated that he had inspected every property. As regards the second question, training requirements were minimal. The task simply entailed testing whether a penknife would penetrate the wood when gentle pressure was applied. The employee had successfully carried out the task previously. He therefore possessed the requisite ability. Management could show that he had been issued with the proper equipment and knew how to use it. Furthermore, he had been allocated ample time to check every property. Had the employee been an unskilled operative it is arguable that supervision was inadequate. Semi-professionals however, can be expected to work unsupervised on a routine job such as this. The employee understood the importance of the work as he was also involved in pricing the contract. No explanation was offered. The employee saw the opportunity for a short cut and took it. Although he received a first warning, a final warning would have been defensible inasmuch as no employer would be prepared to tolerate repetition of the offence. Indeed, dismissal for dishonesty might have been justified.

The second case possesses similar features but the disciplinary issues are more finely balanced:

> A technical assistant was employed to inspect loft conversions in order to certify that the work had been carried out. Certification then enabled the householder to claim a Council grant towards the cost.
>
> The roof of a house collapsed shortly after certification. Inspection revealed sagging timbers and straining joists which, it is alleged, the employee ought to have noticed.
>
> Management intend to dismiss the employee for gross misconduct.

Applying the checklist here yields a markedly different analysis from the preceding case. Management themselves were unable to define the purpose of an inspection. Was it merely to certify that the work had been completed, or was the employee to ensure that it had been carried out to a certain standard? If so, what was the standard? The employee had no training in surveying nor could anyone specify the skills required. The only equipment issued was a note pad which hardly implies that the employee was expected to measure strains, bulges and so forth. The employee worked unsupervised to an unstipulated timescale. He said that he understood his role was to ensure that conversions were *bona fide*. He had never been instructed to inspect the handiwork.

Management argued it was so obviously a 'jerry-built' conversion, that any reasonably alert and conscientious employee 'ought to have known' something was amiss and ought to have drawn it to the householder's attention. The employee had spent less than a minute in the loft. How could this be regarded as exercising reasonable skill and care?

In reaching judgement, you must avoid becoming hypnotised by other people's definitions of reality. Collapse of the roof was a dramatic event accentuated by the householder's threatening to sue the Council for negligence. The latter raised the stakes against the employee but was actually a red herring as the Council was not responsible for the contractor's negligence. Indeed, it was only by chance that the roof collapsed after, and not before, the inspection.

To summarise, this analysis demonstrates that the employee was neither qualified, equipped nor instructed to underwrite the standard of workmanship. Against this is management's argument that a reasonably conscientious person ought to have noticed something amiss and ought to have done something. Had the danger been identified at the inspection, emergency repairs could have been commissioned. Certainly, the employee appeared to have interpreted his role narrowly and might have exercised more initiative. However, this scarcely amounts to gross misconduct. At most, a first warning was justified though management were equally, if not more, at fault for failing to define the job properly in the first place.

Proving that the employee has been properly trained

Training must be carried out and recorded systematically. The following case illustrates the danger of informality.

> A labourer was dismissed for parking his dumper truck unsafely. It had careered down a hill, wrecked three flower beds and demolished an ice-cream hut. At the internal appeal, the trade union representative asked whether the employee had been trained in safe parking procedures? Management replied that he had. When asked to substantiate this however, they could only say that the employee was '... bound to have been shown at some point'.

The employee was reinstated because he could not reasonably be expected to have known what the correct parking procedure was for this specialised piece of equipment and because there was no evidence that he had received proper instruction.

Adequacy of supervision

Disciplinary action is unfair where supervision has been inadequate. The requisite level of oversight depends upon:

- the seniority of the employee;
- the complexity of the task; and
- the experience of the employee.

Generally speaking, the more senior and more experienced an employee the less supervision is required. High task complexity, however, calls for relatively greater supervision.

> A customer was furious after contacting the sales office to speak to the manager. The person who answered replied 'He's out', and put the telephone down.

The telephone had been answered by a trainee, disabled and with severe learning difficulties. The supervisor was at fault for allowing him to take calls without first ensuring that he was competent to do so. The next case is quite different.

> A manager was responsible for submitting quarterly claims for government subsidies. On three successive occasions, he failed to process a claim. Consequently, £1 million were lost. The manager accepted that the task was straightforward and said he had not forgotten about it. He knew he had not made the claims and did not know why.

Although it says little for the organisation's control mechanisms that such a huge shortfall took so long to come to light (and then only when the employee himself casually drew attention to it), it should not detract from the fact that a manager is expected to work with minimal supervision. The employee knew what was required, he offered no excuse and was consequently dismissed for gross misconduct. Why he allowed it to happen is a mystery.

Careful supervision can reduce, but also never eliminate, the potential for human error:

> A machinist was responsible for cutting button holes in jacket sleeves. Ordinary suits have three buttons, dinner jackets only one. The machinist failed to notice that the production line had switched from ordinary suits to dinner jackets and continued therefore, to cut three holes into the sleeves. She had worked through 40 pairs before the mistake was discovered.

Was the employee properly supervised? Sewing 40 pairs of sleeves occupies approximately 20 minutes. The production manager spotted the mistake on his first tour of inspection after lunch, which suggests that supervision was indeed adequate and diligent. The organisation was a small clothing shop and relied mostly on informal methods of maintaining discipline. These were audible half a mile away.

Is the employee under too much pressure?

Mistakes are often attributed to pressure of work. Pressure of work can be caused by one or a combination of the following:

- role ambiguity;

- role strain;

- role overload.

Role ambiguity exists where an employee is uncertain what his job is or how he ought to be carrying it out. Role strain refers to conflict of loyalty — for example when first line supervisors are torn between their duty to behave as managers and the need to relate to the workforce. Fear of asserting authority is a common consequence. Role overload occurs where an employee has more work than he can cope with. It is the most commonly cited form of pressure. In a disciplinary context it is necessary to ascertain whether the claim is valid or merely an excuse. The following checklist provides a framework for a comprehensive investigation and diagnosis.

Checklist for investigating pressure of work

- What do you mean by pressure?

- What, exactly, are you required to do?

- What do each of these tasks involve?

- What systems are utilised?

- How long does each task take?

- Is cooperation from other departments or employees required?

- What is the nature of the working environment? Are there any distractions?

- How are other staff coping?

- Is the problem due to a peak in workload?

- What is your assessment of the employee's emotional state?

Quantity of work is by no means the only potential cause of overload. Poor organisation, inefficient working methods, insufficient or inadequate equipment and the employee's self-organisation and time management are all relevant. Similarly noise, interruptions, and poor seating, workbenches, lighting, heating and ventilation can impede progress resulting in overload. The employee's personal well-being can significantly affect his perceptions and ability to cope.

Employee counselling

Counselling skills are beyond the scope of this book. Many excellent texts and training courses are available and you are recommended to acquire some basic knowledge. It is your responsibility as manager, however, to be alert to the onset of psychological problems. Any of the following are worth gentle enquiry:

- A deterioration in performance of a hitherto satisfactory employee.

- Withdrawal or apathy, such as loss of interest in work and other employees.

- Physical changes, including weight loss; signs of strain in the eyes or face; shaking and changes in body posture.

- Behavioural changes, for instance deterioration in standards of dress, appearance and time keeping; unexplained disappearances from the work place.

- Sudden requests for leave or an increase in sickness absence.

The following points are not a substitute for training in counselling skills but may be useful.

- Patience, gentleness and sensitivity are essential in building rapport.

- An indirect approach is sometimes helpful, for example 'I wish I could lose weight like that. How do you do it?'

- Once an employee starts talking, keep him talking, if necessary, about anything.

- Once a dialogue is under way, remember it may take time for the employee to confide in you.

- If you know that the employee is receiving medication or treatment, talk to him about it. There is nothing wrong in asking what the doctor said, whether the tablets are doing any good and so on.

- If the employee is hesitant, at least let him know that he can come to you whenever he wishes.

Life traumas such as bereavement and divorce can destroy powers of concentration. Consequently symptoms of stress, anxiety or depression, are easily mis-diagnosed as disciplinary problems.

The performance of a medical records officer gradually deteriorated. Files were lost, forms were left uncompleted and so on. Eventually, relations between the employee and his supervisor broke down. Attempts to mediate were unsuccessful and, therefore, the employee was offered a transfer to another department. He declined and was then sent a letter instructing him to attend a disciplinary hearing a few days hence. The employee then went home, saying he was ill. On the morning of the hearing, he committed suicide.

Although it was the disgrace of facing a hearing which precipitated suicide, the employee actually obtained the sleeping pills used to kill himself shortly after his partner had deserted him four years earlier. The signs of depression — dramatic weight loss, neglect of personal appearance, withdrawn behaviour, and inability to concentrate — had long been visible yet no one interpreted them correctly.

Finally, it is emphasised that poor performance is not the only factor associated with depression and suicide:

A highly competent and well-regarded senior manager took four bottles of paracetamol and a bottle of whisky to a lonely spot from which he never returned. His suicide note said that he felt a failure in his job.

It was subsequently learned that the employee was being treated for depression at the time of his suicide. Over the last month or two of his life, a few of his memoranda had been incoherent but no conclusions were drawn from this. Colleagues noted that the manager had often suggested going to lunch but it was assumed that he was simply being pleasant and sociable. None guessed that he might have been anxious to talk to someone. As regards the manager's performance, why he saw himself as a failure was unimaginable, except perhaps that no one had ever given him any feedback whatsoever.

Dealing with long-standing performance problems

Despite the fact that an employee has 'been like that for years', it is never too late to interpose. Simply make it clear that prevailing norms are unacceptable, and specify how these must change. Beware of trying to spare the employee's feelings by suggesting that new standards now apply as he may respond by demanding an increase in pay. Broach the issue uncritically by saying something like 'One of the things we need to change is . . .'. Tact, however, should never defer to firmness. A grossly under-employed cleaner once said to a new manager 'It sounds like you're giving me more work'. Had he agreed with this observation, he would have been drawn into a series of arguments. Instead, he replied 'You may see it that way. I don't. I see it as you doing the job you're paid to do'.

Personality clashes

While inter-personal relations are employees' own business, they become a management concern if they impinge upon work. Personality clashes may be overcome by voluntary transfer of one or both parties. Where, however, protagonists must work together, both must observe the minimum standards of behaviour operationally necessary. Never become involved in the conflict itself. Focus solely upon the consequences.

Two factory operatives had not spoken to one another for 20 years. The method of production changed and consequently, both employees were required to communicate and cooperate with one another in order to maintain the work flow. Each blamed the other for failing to do so. Baskets of materials piled up, orders were delayed and other workers became upset as their piecework earnings were affected.

As with any potential disciplinary case, the first step is to investigate. Investigation should seek to establish:

1. How the parties are behaving towards one another.
2. How each of the parties is behaving towards other people.
3. The consequences of both parties' behaviour.

Conflict is reciprocal and usually both parties are to blame to some degree, therefore both should be warned. Again, subject to proper investigation, dismissal of both employees would be fair if warnings were unsuccessful. Where one party is demonstrably more at fault, it may be reasonable to dismiss him and warn the other.

Clashes between groups of staff are also a management concern as, typically, much energy is expended in conflict over trivial issues.

Personnel and Training shared a Christmas tree. Every year, there was an argument over where to site it. Eventually, it was agreed that the tree should be placed exactly on the borderline of the two sections. Training then moved to another floor and demanded either the tree or their money back. Personnel were so disgusted, they paid them out in halfpennies.

Team building can be extremely effective in enabling groups to modify their behaviour. Hostility feeds on fear and unwarranted assumptions about what other people are thinking, doing and feeling. Communications with one another, therefore, in a structured and constructive environment can achieve change deeper and more lasting than exhortation or discipline.

Professional performance

The literature of organisations is rich in debate over the definition of professions and professionals. The arguments are irrelevant here because professionals are accountable in the same way as other employees. The idea that intervention is a slur upon someone's 'professionalism', whatever that means, is a nonsense. Similarly, the notion that investigation of professional conduct by non-professionals is outrageous, intolerable and slanderous, is bluster. The lecturer who fails to turn up for classes; the doctor who is rude to a patient; the lawyer who is negligent are all guilty of misconduct. The best advice therefore, if you are called upon to deal with disciplinary matters concerning professional staff, is to avoid being drawn into arguments over professionalism. If challenged, stress that you are concerned solely with misconduct.

It is an abdication of managerial responsibility to allow professional staff to work unsupervised and uncontrolled. One hears 'He's a professional, he knows what to do, he will do it'. Indemnity insurance would not exist if these assumptions were warranted. Professional staff may be required to conform to standards of output, timekeeping and so forth in the same way as other employees. Indeed, in law, professionals have higher obligations than other employees. Whereas a labourer, for example, may do extra work on an overtime basis, professionals have a duty to finish a task however long it means them working.

Performance standards are more clearly defined for many professionals than for other categories of staff. This makes it more difficult for the employee to argue that he was unaware of what was required of him. For example:

> A solicitor responsible for a property transaction failed to inform his client of a right of way through the garden. This was discovered when the client came to sell the house, the value of which was consequently reduced.

The right of way was clear in the deed. Since there could be no doubt that the solicitor's role was to scrutinise the documentation, he had clearly committed misconduct by failing to exercise reasonable thoroughness and diligence.

Managerial performance

A commonly-held misconception is that managerial performance is complex and therefore difficult to address. The following model demonstrates how managerial roles and performance expectations can be defined, and how achievements can be assessed. Essentially, this involves establishing:

- what the manager has done; and

- whether it has been effective.

It was emphasised in the last chapter that the first step in dealing with performance problems is to define the employee's role. It is appreciated that good job descriptions at this level are rare. However, common factors exist between managerial jobs and are used here as a basis for analysing performance.

Senior management

At the highest level, managers are typically responsible for strategy. Key responsibilities are:

- Directing general policy and the coordination of strategy.

- Ensuring competitiveness and future viability of the organisation.

- Enhancing the image of the organisation.

- Preparation, control and monitoring of the business plan.

- The attainment of organisational objectives.

Performance can be assessed by selective use and adaptation of the following checklist.

Checklist for assessing performance of senior management

- What have you done to achieve ...?
- What were your key objectives?
- How were these formulated?
- How did you propose to implement the changes that were necessary?
- How was this enacted?
- What assumptions were made?
- How were these justified?
- How did you propose to obtain cooperation from other departments?
- What was the result?
- How did you approach/formulate/implement ...
- What performance indicators did you monitor to ensure viability?
- How did you analyse/evaluate/review these?
- What obstacles were identified?
- What plans existed to overcome these?
- What has been achieved?
- How have you evaluated whether you have been successful?
- What is your future strategy for this work?

Set out in advance the level of answer expected. For example, a first or second-tier manager would probably be expected to produce a detailed organisational strategy containing long, medium and short-term objectives with the rationale for change clearly identified. You would expect clear statements on how objectives be achieved and an analysis of the implications for all parts of the organisation, such as personnel, production and marketing. Options should be formulated and evaluated comprehensively. Recommendations should be clear, realistic and consistent with the argument.

Similarly, you must know what you expect the manager to achieve. When you say 'Promote the image of the department', do you mean that he should have organised a stall at a local show and had a few posters printed or were you expecting a comprehensive, clearly thought out public relations strategy and action plan? Ask the manager 'What have you done?' and measure the answers against your expectations. Vague responses such as 'Quite a lot really . . . have made every effort . . . done everything possible' are inadequate. A clear vision of expectations is also necessary when exploring the reasons for the deficiencies. It is reasonable for example, to expect assertiveness and political skill at senior level. If the manager says that other departments failed to cooperate, he should be asked how he planned and executed his approach and why it was ineffective.

An analysis such as this is extremely powerful in that it highlights the extent to which a manager has managed in the first place. In other words, your case is strengthened exponentially by your being able to show that not only has the manager failed to attain key objectives, but that his whole approach to the task was inadequate and, therefore, doomed to failure.

Middle and junior managerial performance

Middle and junior managers exercise similar functions for the control of sectors of the organisation, varying mainly in the scale of their respective responsibilities. Commonly, these include:

- cost control;

- attainment of profit targets;

- monitoring of productivity and quality;

- control, motivation and direction of staff;

- ensuring adherence to organisational procedures such as for invoicing, banking of cash and stock control;

- maintenance of good industrial relations;

- planning, including programming workload, ensuring availability of materials and other resources;

- staff recruitment and discipline;

- contributing to the development of policy;

- collaboration with other departments and organisations; and

- reviewing effectiveness.

Again, performance must be measured against expectations. Effective cost control, for example, requires utilisation and verification of relevant information, monitoring and appropriate intervention. Performance can be assessed by asking:

1. What information is utilised?
2. How is this obtained?
3. What is its quality?
4. How do you know?
5. How up-to-date is it?
6. Where is it kept?
7. In what form is it kept? Is it easy to interpret, for example?
8. What are the criteria for action?
9. How is it acted upon?
10. What are the results?

A building contract was a year behind schedule. The site agent responsible for managing had no project management schedules. Consequently, it was impossible to tell which tasks had been completed, which remained and in what order they would be accomplished. This meant that no one could reliably predict when the building would be completed.

The site agent said he 'did not believe in charts and things'. He attributed the delays to shortages of key trades, failure to deliver materials on time and the fact that the men were on fixed wages instead of bonus and, therefore, had no incentive to work hard.

To ask if the manager is to blame poses the wrong question. The issue is whether, despite setbacks, the manager has performed adequately? The first step is to eliminate extraneous factors as follows:

● Given that key tradesmen could not be recruited on time and given that deliveries were late, what pressure did the manager exert on the personnel office and suppliers respectively? Second, what contingency plans did he make, and were these optimal in the circumstances?

● Given that no bonus scheme existed, what had the manager done to press for change? Second, in view of the lack of incentives, what control did he adopt?

When one moves onto the manager's performance in controlling and scheduling work, the following question and answer session ensued:

Q. What was your original project plan?
A. Should have been finished last May.

Q. How was this revised when it became apparent that the completion date was hopelessly unattainable?

A. We just did our best, managed to keep the lads going.

Q. When is the building now expected to be completed?
A. Next May.

Q. How has this date been arrived at?
A. Well, it isn't going to be any sooner.

Q. What formal project planning has taken place?
A. Waste of time that.

Q. What potentially critical events have been identified?
A. If the paving stones arrive we shall be all right.

Q. What alternatives are scheduled if plans now break down at a critical point?
A. I shall just have to see.

Notwithstanding factors over which he had no direct control, but could have exerted influence, the manager is clearly failing to exercise his fundamental responsibilities for controlling and directing the project. The result is a costly shambles. Indeed, a year later the building remains unfinished. Perhaps, though, one might now ask why the site agent's own manager has failed to intervene earlier and insist that the manager adopt proper methods of control in accordance with the training he has received?

A similar approach can be applied to less tangible aspects of performance such as motivating and directing staff. Again, essentially you are seeking to know what the manager has done. Are staff meetings held, for example? Do employees work to clear objectives? How often does the manager spend time with them? Does he know what motivates the individuals under his control, and how does he know?

Summary and checklist

- Incompetents lack essential skills and abilities. They tend to be recruited as a result of unwarranted assumptions about transferability of skills.

- The longer an employee stays in a post the harder it becomes to argue he is incompetent. Signs of incompetence should, therefore, be acted upon immediately.

- At senior levels, the first submission of a substantial piece of written work is a reliable predictor of competence. An unsatisfactory submission should be systematically appraised and investigated.

- Ill health dismissals are not disciplinary matters. However, the relationship between performance and ill health is reciprocal and it is important to ascertain which precedes which in the causal chain.

- Employees suffering from alcoholism should not be dismissed if they are willing to accept treatment.

- Incapability can result from organisational change such as the introduction of new technology.

- The exercise of skill and care imply concentration, diligence, adherence to working methods and standards, and use of initiative.

- Disciplinary cases involving failure to exercise skill and care often turn on whether the employee was properly trained and instructed.

- Training must be formally carried out and recorded.

- Supervision must be adequate. Generally speaking, the more senior the employee, the less supervision is required. Task complexity requires relatively greater supervision.

- Professionals are accountable and may be managed in the same way as other employees. Performance standards, however, are often higher and duties more clearly defined.

- Never become involved in arguments over 'professionalism'. Concentrate upon misconduct.

- Senior managers are usually responsible for strategy; middle and junior managers for control of a sector of the organisation.

- Performance at all managerial levels depends on what the manager has done, and whether it has been effective. A critical determinant of effectiveness is the manner in which the manager has approached the task.

Chapter Five
Refusal to Carry Out Instructions

Introduction

The legal background

An employee is expected to obey his employer. Disobedience constitutes gross misconduct as, clearly, the employee is destroying the *raison d'être* for his employment. This general principle however assumes:

- The employer's instruction is lawful.

- The instruction falls within the scope of the employee's contract.

- The employee has been made aware that he is jeopardising his employment by refusing to obey.

Lawful means an employee cannot, for example, be required to drive a vehicle which has bald tyres or to sell illegal drugs or substances. *Within the scope of an employee's contract* means that an unqualified nurse for instance, may legitimately refuse to administer injections or treatments which are beyond his responsibilities. On the third point, an employee should always be asked why he is unwilling to obey and should be given the opportunity to retract, either through informal discussion and persuasion, or, if necessary, by means of a formal warning.

A grave-digger distressed relatives of the bereaved by producing graves coffin-shaped. He was instructed by management to dig them oblong. Despite warnings, he persisted in furnishing a casket-shaped variety.

All three conditions are met here. The instruction was lawful and well within the scope of the grave-digger's contract. His intransigence reflected the fact that digging graves coffin-shaped saves effort. Persuasion failed and therefore the employee was formally warned that unless he complied he would be sacked, as eventually he was.

Dealing with disobedience in practice

The exercise of legal rights is often constrained by trade union intervention. Conflict commonly centres upon whether the instruction is consistent with the employee's contract of employment. Moreover, it is important to be mindful that an employee refusing to obey has committed himself and may be unwilling to change his mind for fear of losing face.

An important role of the manager is to make it easy for the employee to acquiesce. Judgement and sensitivity are necessary in order to decide whether it is appropriate to respond quickly, firmly and decisively, or whether a persuasive or non-reactive approach is best. Much of this chapter is therefore devoted to tactics. It is impossible to cover every conceivable situation but it is hoped that the examples which follow are sufficiently typical and comprehensive to enable the reader to gain an insight into how to handle problems. Never lose sight of the fact that ultimately you have a right and a duty to manage. The aim here is to show how power and authority can be exercised effectively and confidently.

Dealing with outright refusal

Disobedience is defined as an employee's refusal to discharge any aspect of his role, be it:

- a particular task at a particular time;

- all or part of his job;

- compliance with specific instructions;

- the acceptance of new responsibilities.

The counter-response: 'you will'

Sometimes an unequivocal response is essential to prevent individual disobedience from degenerating into general anarchy such as in this case.

> Some butchery workers were seen by their supervisor loading meat into a van at the supermarket where they worked. Their supervisor reported this to the supermarket manager but said if it came to a disciplinary hearing, he would deny it.

Managing difficult staff

To begin with, the supervisor's performance is unimpressive. He should have challenged the employees while they were loading the van. Moreover, regardless of what his job description says, the supervisor is potentially guilty of disobedience in seeking to evade the fundamental responsibilities of his role. Staff supervision implies a duty to report subordinates' misdeeds, and to participate in the disciplinary process. As he is probably motivated by fear, the most effective response is to say 'you will' and close the discussion. If necessary, the manager should then indicate the possible consequences of failure to comply. The initial fear will then be replaced by a worse one. Incidentally, if the supervisor ultimately refused to cooperate, the manager could give hearsay evidence against the butchery workers.

Preventing escalation

During World War II a naval captain knew he risked mutiny if he ordered his exhausted crew to clear the decks. Although a court martial would have supported him in this, nevertheless, he and his first lieutenant went out on deck and started moving the equipment themselves. Realising the importance of the task, the crew soon joined in.

This case illustrates how potentially serious disciplinary situations can be avoided by exemplary management rather than by reliance upon formal authority. Other preventive tactics include:

- ignoring the situation;
- studied unawareness; and
- seeking to understand 'the problem'.

These are ranked in ascending order, beginning with the least reactive responses.

Ignoring the situation

Although ostensibly an abdication of managerial responsibility, this is a wise tactic because, as the gesture is unacknowledged, the employee can retract without losing face. Furthermore, non-reaction sows doubt. The employee begins to wonder whether he can, after all, predict events, should be continue to defy. Another way of surprising the employee is to announce 'I no longer require you to undertake this task. I will do it myself'. Obviously this tactic should be used sparingly. However, ignoring someone in this way can be more effective in the long run than confrontation.

Studied unawareness

Never ask an employee why he is 'refusing' to do something. Begin instead by appearing a little slow on the uptake by enquiring whether there is a problem. This immediately allows the employee to extricate himself if he perceives that he has acted foolishly or impulsively. If, for example, he replies 'No, I just wasn't sure what to do', simply nod and say 'OK now?'

Seeking to understand the problem

A parks' manager requires advice. One of his labourers is refusing to use a grass-cutting machine and he has no other work for him. The manager wants to know whether he should send the labourer home and call a disciplinary hearing the next day.

Although the manager's suggestion is legally defensible, it should only be used as a last resort. Faced with a problem such as this he should:

- talk to the employee privately;

- explore his concerns;

- ascertain specifically what it is he is unwilling to do and why; and

- seek a positive way forward.

It is essential to speak out of sight of other employees and in an atmosphere conducive to calm and rational discussion. Privacy is essential to prevent others from joining and provoking the conflict. If an employee is aggressive, send him home and meet next day. Refusals are often a 'last straw' response to tension which is usually unconcerned with the task itself, relations with a supervisor or unfair treatment. A broadly-based discussion is therefore required.

Identifying the real problem provides the opportunity for the employee to retract with dignity. For instance, in this case he may say 'It's not that I'm unwilling to use the grass cutter, I just feel that . . .'.

Remain firm on the principle that an employee must carry out all reasonable instructions. A positive way forward is one which reconciles individual and organisational aspirations, in this case perhaps an agreement that the labourer will cut the grass and the manager will review the rota to achieve a more equitable distribution of work.

Sometimes it is necessary to redefine a problem in order to make progress. For example:

An apprentice refused to sweep the floor because he felt he was being singled out for demeaning work because he was black. The problem came to a head because his parents were furious when he told them. They had expected their son to be trained as an engineer.

Ostensibly, resistance here stems from perceived discrimination. The real problem, however, is that the apprentice has been influenced by his parents, whose expectations are unrealistic, as all apprentices are required to sweep the floor.

Discussion should focus less upon the legitimacy of the instruction and more upon the apprentice's parents, their aspirations and influence upon him. The manager cannot make an exception of the apprentice, but he can help him to adjust his expectations. Given a little time and patience, the youth will probably see for himself that exemption would set him apart from his fellows, which is the last thing he wants.

A strategy for applying power

Swift resort to disciplinary action in cases of disobedience may be legally defensible. However, it leaves management vulnerable to accusations of over-reacting and heavy-handed behaviour. Furthermore, if sanctions fail — for instance your own manager refuses to support you or the trade unions invoke a grievance against you — there are no options left. Persuasion is seldom effective once coercion has been applied. Power is best applied slowly, beginning with the least drastic of responses and gradually tightening control.

A good example of this strategy in action is President Kennedy's handling of the Cuban Missile Crisis. Two options were identified; to impose a naval blockade round Cuba to prevent further military supplies reaching the island; or to destroy the missile bases by an air strike. Opponents of the blockade argued that it was a weak response given the gravity of the situation. Supporters argued that it had the advantage in that the restricted zone could be tightened if the situation worsened, and, more particularly, it still left the option of carrying out an air attack. Although the latter had the advantage of providing a swift and decisive response, at the very least it would be provocative. Worse, if it failed, and the risk was significant, escalation would be the only option left.

Signalling power

Power exists where A *believes* that B possesses the intention and capability of applying sanctions. Often, power is greater when applied indirectly. After President Kennedy imposed the blockade, he deliberately stopped a neutral ship rather than a Russian one from entering the restricted zone. That way, he conveyed his intentions to the Soviets, yet avoided a confrontation.

If this approach is applied to the workplace, power can be mobilised by signals such as 'I would be reluctant to have to instruct you'. This clearly shows that your authority is intact and implies that there is an alternative to persuasion, yet it spares the employee the ignominy of forced compliance. If necessary, you can tighten your grasp by pointing out 'You realise if this goes on, I will have no alternative but to instruct you formally'. Remember however the importance of saving face. An employee's intransigence may reflect fear of climbing down and appearing foolish. Your role is to make acquiesence easy. If someone is in a deep hole, throw him a ladder. An employee may say 'I'll do it if . . .' or 'Can I have . . .' and make some inconsequential request. Just reply 'Sure'. In other words, as the former TUC leader Vic Feather used to say, 'Always leave the other person with his bus fare home'.

The technique of persusasion

Allowing time for reflection is the key to effective persuasion. Breaking off the discussion lifts the pressure and gives the employee space to reassess his position and see for himself that resistance is futile. It may also enable him to find a way of complying without sacrificing dignity.

The signal may be oblique. For example, the employee may organise something connected with the task as a way of communicating acquiesence without actually saying so directly. Similarly it is important to be alert to subtle changes in the employee's expressions, attitudes or behaviour. Initial arrogance or defiance may give way to doubt as power is applied and as the employee comes to realise the folly of his intransigence.

Where the employee has a grievance

> A manager was asked to assume overall responsibility for the nightshift. He refused, saying that it was not in his job description. A restructuring exercise then took place and this responsibility was included in all job descriptions at this level. Still the manager refused. The reasons he gave were unclear. He said that he had not been consulted about the change; colleagues in personnel had failed to reply to enquiries; these were unconnected with the issue; he received 'no support'; and so on.

The existence of a grievance is a common reason for disobedience. Some grievances are genuine. Often, however, they are used to evade compliance by causing delay, confusion and distraction. Arguably, the existence of a grievance is irrelevant to carrying out instructions, provided these meet the conditions set out at the beginning of this chapter. Tactically, however, where practicable, it is best to deal with the grievance before enforcing obedience.

Even where a grievance is obviously fatuous, it should be heard formally. This is because:

- It forces the employee to identify all of his concerns.

- If the concerns are fatuous, airing them in a formal hearing will expose them as such.

- The hearing enables management to respond formally and forcefully to the employee.

- Processing the issue within procedure provides proof of reasonable behaviour by management.

- The hearing provides a basis for the next step.

Briefly, containment is the key to managing conflict. While an employee has a grievance, he is in control. The objective in putting the issue in procedure is less about solving a grievance and more about taking charge. We now examine how this works in practice.

> I refer to our meeting on Tuesday where we discussed the transfer of responsibility for nightshift to middle managers. You said that you were unwilling to undertake this role because of a number of unresolved issues. I understood you to mean that you wish to discuss a formal grievance. If so, please would you confirm within seven days and I will arrange a hearing

in accordance with the Grievance Procedure as set out in the Employee Handbook.

This document is a deliberate power play. It obliquely indicates management's determination to obtain compliance and signals to the employee that persuasion is about to cease. By forcing him to 'Put up or shut up', as the saying goes, this letter removes control from the employee who has, so far, used innuendo to dissuade management from exerting authority. Incidentally, it should be emphasised to the manager that all his grievances must be put. There can be no question of his trying to protract matters by returning with further complaints later. If he declines to present a grievance he should be instructed to comply with whatever is required. It is important that the invitation is put in writing as this prevents the employee from claiming subsequently that he never had the opportunity to be heard.

The outcome of the hearing should be confirmed in writing as follows:

1. The background to the problem.
2. The concerns raised by the employee.
3. Management's response to each of the employee's concerns.
4. The action now required from the employee.

Here, for example, the letter might read:

Dear

①→ You stated that you were unwilling to manage the nightshift because:

    i   you have not been consulted over the change in responsibilities;
    ii certain correspondence from yourself to the personnel depart-
②→   ment have not been answered;
    iii you have received insufficient support from senior management.

③→ I find the first of these points untenable. While it is true that formal consultation did not take place, you were well aware of the proposal. The Division's management team minutes indicate that the issue was discussed there on no fewer than seven occasions and you were present each time.

Your second point is irrelevant. The correspondence you referred to concern payment of wages and I cannot see how the absence of a response prevents you from taking responsibility for the nightshift.

The third point, I understand, reflects your general feeling that management are insufficiently firm in their dealings with the trade unions. Since you produced no evidence to substantiate this profit, I must dismiss it.

In summary, I find no reason why you cannot or should not undertake responsibility for the nightshift. I shall now expect you to perform this duty henceforth. I trust now that your grievances have been resolved, you will proceed with this task. I must emphasise, however, that further resistance will be treated as a disciplinary matter.

④ →

Yours sincerely

As this case shows, sometimes it is necessary for an employee to express his grievances in order to see for himself that they are fatuous. If disciplinary action is required, these letters are evidence that the employee has had full opportunity to air his concerns and that time and effort have been spent in persuasion, which has clearly failed. The reference to disciplinary action at the end of the second letter is important. Never assume that the employee already knows the potential consequences of disobedience. He may well believe he possesses more power than he actually has. In any case, it is essential to prove that the employee had been well warned.

Issuing an instruction

'He keeps on saying he won't do it. What shall I do?' The answer is simple. Stop asking. There comes a point where progress ceases. You have asked politely. You have listened to the employee and have done everything you can to solve his problems. You have asked again, still politely, and still he refuses. You ask once more. Once more he refuses. Clearly, it is pointless to continue asking. You must change your approach. Next time, don't ask, instruct.

Issuing an instruction represents a watershed. Persuasion is now at an end and the employee is presented with a clear choice. Either he does what is required of him, or he takes the consequences. No one can accuse you of behaving precipitously or of over-reacting as you can demonstrate that you behaved reasonably. It is the employee who has left you with no choice.

Even at this late stage, leave room for the employee to retract by first issuing the instruction verbally.

Jim, I am now instructing you to write the piece of software requested by the purchasing department. You must understand that if you now refuse to carry out this work, I will have no alternative but to call you to a disciplinary hearing. You should also understand that if you continue to refuse, you will eventually be dismissed. I hope, however, that now having made your point about the running of the organisation, which incidentally I value, you will now see why it is necessary to utilise your skills and expertise in this important task. I am looking forward to discussing the outline specification with you next Wednesday.

This message achieves several important purposes:

- Jim now sees his manager is serious.

- The consequences of failing to comply are clear.

- Jim's views on the organisation are taken seriously. This makes Jim feel valued. It also makes his resistance seem foolish whereas his manager appears reasonable.

- Jim is given time in which to accept the situation. The specification is deliberately not required for some days hence.

- Treating the issue as an engaging professional discussion allows Jim to save face.

If Jim asks for written instructions, treat the request as a face-saver and respond accordingly. Similarly a reply 'I can't do it for Wednesday', is also a face-saver. It clearly indicates a shift in Jim's position yet allows him to maintain the *appearance* of retaining some control. If the response is ambiguous, behave as if it is positive. Jim may need you to make the decision for him.

If Jim's response is negative, do not argue but confirm the instruction in writing. This gives Jim one last chance. Written communication often has more impact than verbal delivery.

Finally *never* show triumph when the employee does comply. Quiet acceptance is sufficient. If you humiliate the employee, he will remember. All managers rely upon subordinates' cooperation and sometimes need them to go beyond the call of duty. Besides, the most junior subordinate can undermine his superior through misrepresentation, malicious gossip and innuendo. Be mindful too, of the old adage about kicking people on the way up whom you might meet on your way down!

'It's not in my job description'

This is a common but rarely valid reason for refusal. The function of a job description is to outline the major tasks and responsibilities of a postholder. Job descriptions are far from being legally solemnised documents. Provided an instruction is within the scope of the employee's responsibilities, it is immaterial whether it is specified in the job description, as the following example shows.

> A new manager asked his personal assistant/secretary to take dictation by shorthand. She refused saying that it was not in her job description. Furthermore, she pointed out that in the seven years she had been in post, she had steadfastly refused to take shorthand.

Although the job description contained no reference to shorthand, one of the main tasks of the postholder was 'To provide a confidential secretarial service'. It was difficult to see how this could be provided without the facility of shorthand or dictation equipment, which the secretary also declined to use, though she was capable of both. The reason was she felt it demeaning for a personal assistant to take dictation. This, however, was unreasonable as both job title and job description indicate a substantial element of secretarial duties. It was irrelevant that previous managers resorted to handwriting. They should have insisted upon dictation.

Some cases are more open to interpretation:

> A group of grave-diggers objected to carrying out exhumations. These involved exposure to putrid and often liquid remains resulting from spades penetrating rotten chipboard.

The grave-diggers' main role was described in their job description as 'The digging, preparation and infill of graves'. One of the tasks listed referred to the re-opening of graves for further burials. Management argued that this implied exhumations. The trade unions maintained that these were beyond the scope of a grave-digger's role. The problem was resolved by the trade unions' accepting the principle that exhumations were part of the grave-digger's role, and by management's accepting that, as the task was so unpleasant, a special payment of £75 per exhumation was justified.

The case of the 'Special Services Unit', however, is different:

The Unit was employed to de-fumigate and clean properties. All prospective employees were told that the work regularly involved contact with human and animal remains. For example, the Unit was deployed following murder cases and operatives were expected to wash walls covered in blood and remove brain tissue from furniture and other surfaces.

A dispute arose when the Unit refused to remove syringes from properties vacated by drug addicts. They claimed that their job description did not cover such a potentially dangerous task.

Management rejected the demand for an additional payment on the basis that, provided protective clothing was worn and safety procedures observed, the risks were negligible compared to the health hazards regularly encountered by the Unit. In other words, the task was consistent with the scope and general nature of the operative's role even though it was not actually specified within the job description. Incidentally, this argument is valid where no job descriptions exist.

Exposure to danger

An employee may not be required to undertake work exposing him to danger. If faced with a refusal to comply for this reason, the critical question is whether the employee is exposed to danger. For example:

A group of workmen refused to commence alterations to a building because the structure contained asbestos.

Although it was true that the structure of the building did indeed contain asbestos, there was no risk of actual exposure and therefore no danger. The next case was different:

A gang of electricians was rewiring a block of multi-storey flats in an inner-city area known to be populated by drug addicts and criminals. As they were working, someone hurled a motorcycle from the balcony. It missed them by fewer than three feet.

Work was rightly postponed until cover could be provided. Had the gang then refused to continue working, they would have been guilty of disobedience if management could show that conditions were now safe.

Danger can arise where the employee is not fully competent to perform a particular task. For instance:

A demolition worker was required to work in a cooling tower contaminated with asbestos. His employer argued that the instruction was reasonable in that employees' contracts of employment required them to undertake alternative duties when their regular work was unavailable. Proper safety equipment was provided. The employee refused because the work involved was that of an asbestos technician and he had not been trained for that work.

Asbestos removal is a specialist task and can only be carried out under licence. Licences are only issued to contractors capable of meeting stringent safety requirements. There is a high risk of an accident occurring where someone is unfamiliar with safe working practices and safe use of equipment. Therefore the employee here was potentially exposed to danger.

Exposure to danger covers a wide range of circumstances. A further example is given below.

A clerk working alone in a social services office on a housing estate was confronted by an angry parent demanding to know when his daughter would be released from care. The clerk said she was unable to help and gave him the number of the appropriate department. The man screwed up the paper saying he wasn't 'interested in no f...... other department' and said if he couldn't see his daughter tomorrow, he would return and beat her head in with an axe.

The man had a history of criminal violence and was believed to be a heroin user. Management argued that imposing physical barriers added to clients' feelings of alienation and helplessness. The trade unions, however, saw it differently. They insisted that access to the building be controlled, no one be allowed to work alone and a reliable alarm system be installed.

The importance of listening

It was noted earlier in this chapter that it is essential to ascertain the reasons for an employee's unwillingness to comply. The importance of listening cannot be over-emphasised. Beware of misinterpreting genuine concern as insubordination.

A headteacher bought a printing machine from another school for £1,000. Congratulating himself upon acquiring such a splendid bargain, he duly installed it in the stock cupboard and instructed a Mrs Fisher, the clerk, to use it. Mrs Fisher demurred as the room had no ventilation or natural light and there was barely room for her and the machine. Relations between clerk and headteacher were strained in any case and the headteacher interpreted Mrs Fisher's objections as yet another display of hostility. He therefore ordered her to work the machine.

When school ended, Mrs Fisher emerged from the cupboard, half anaesthetised by fumes, her print dress ruined by black ink leaking from the machine. The headteacher was unsympathetic and said it was her fault for operating the machine incorrectly. This was the last straw. In desperation, Mrs Fisher telephoned her trade union. An immediate inspection by local authority safety officers followed. They condemned the machine and told the headteacher that it must not be used without modifications to the room. These would cost him £5,000.

The un-cooperative employee

Motivating un-cooperative employees

Un-cooperative employees are defined as those stopping short of open defiance, but who impede the organisation by causing difficulties and disruption. Un-cooperative employees are sometimes regarded as problematic because, it is said, their attitude is at fault. Since attitudes are intangible, sanctions are seldom applied. This is a misconception because what we term 'attitudes' are actually behaviours if examined carefully. Behaviour can be defined and changed either through motivation and reward, or by punishment. Many excellent texts on motivation are available and it is beyond the scope of this book to attempt to summarise the subject. Much of the theorising and research suggest, however, that hostility can be reduced by making people feel valued. For example:

- Share your plans and information. This makes the employee feel knowledgeable and so reduces the feelings of powerlessness.

Managing difficult staff

- Identify and capitalise upon an employee's talents. Let him lead from strength.

- Show that you understand and appreciate an employee's special abilities. You might for example say 'This job requires a lot of detailed figure work, I thought you might enjoy it'.

- By sounding excited and committed yourself, you will stimulate excitement and commitment in others.

- Discover what motivates individuals and manipulate rewards accordingly.

- Close discussions with a commitment to action.

- Unceasing praise may be viewed suspiciously by employees, otherwise be generous with warmth and appreciation. They stimulate effort and cost nothing.

Countering un-cooperative employees directly

Motivation will not always succeed. A drastic counter-response can be an extremely effective means of asserting authority. Interestingly, where a firm approach is taken at the outset, many potential mavericks see that they are wasting their time and either leave or get on with the job. Some may feel more secure and therefore happier through having their role clearly defined. Some may even shine.

Putting an un-cooperative employee on the defensive

This gambit is useful with employees who are intentionally negative, particularly in a group situation. The aim is to put the employee on the defensive by returning the challenge. For example:

- 'Peter, why do you think the idea is complete rubbish?'

- 'Peter thinks the idea is complete rubbish, Jim, what do you think?' or 'What do the rest of you think?'

- 'Peter, if this idea is complete rubbish, how do you propose to solve the problem?'

- 'What do the rest of you think about Peter's idea?'

- 'Peter, when can we see your ideas set out in detail so that we can compare options?'

- 'Peter, were you trying to be positive when you said . . .?'

By now, if Peter was behaving negatively, he will be wishing he had kept quiet. If his criticism was genuinely constructive, he will be pleased it has been taken seriously.

Changing un-cooperative employees' behaviour

Lack of co-operation can become so habitual that the employee may lose sight of how he is perceived. The technique is to observe him and note his behaviour. For example, every time he grumbles, responds negatively or has to be chased to produce work, write it down. After say six or seven significant instances have accumulated, discuss the problem with the employee. Remember, *never* get into arguments about attitudes — focus upon behaviour. Explain your concerns and substantiate these with your examples. Indicate the type of behaviour that is expected.

Always listen to the employee, but bear in mind that you need not be defensive about things you cannot change. Nor need you commit yourself to finding the employee more interesting or better-paid work, or arranging early retirement on enhanced terms. You have a responsibility towards all of your staff, the remainder of whom may be quietly getting on with their work. Beware of paying undue attention to those who happen to complain most loudly. Do what you reasonably can to help the employee, but make it clear his behaviour must change forthwith and unconditionally.

Applying the disciplinary process to un-cooperative employees

Some employees are un-cooperative to the point of deliberately seeking to undermine managerial authority. Since they will transgress as far as they think safe, your strategy must be to allow them ample scope and then to choose an opportunity to intervene. There will probably be plenty of potential opportunities. The key to effectiveness is to focus upon:

- the most serious;
- one where the employee is unambiguously at fault; and
- the one which carries the least risk of a successful defence at a disciplinary hearing.

For example:

A word processor operator working in a pool of staff deliberately distressed her supervisor by making rude and personal comments about her to other staff. She also had a habit of deriding a colleague who was disabled, again, not directly, but sufficiently loudly to discomfit the employee and other members of staff. Moreover, she was an unwilling worker.

Her supervisor was in a dilemma as he felt that if he remonstrated with the employee, she would claim victimisation.

This case contains three potential disciplinary issues, namely:

1. The employee's behaviour towards her supervisor.
2. Her behaviour towards her disabled colleague.
3. Her unwillingness to work.

The best one to focus upon initially is the employee's behaviour towards her disabled colleague. This is both serious and inexcusable. It carries less risk of a counter-claim of victimisation than the other issues as it is not directly concerned with the employee's relationship with her supervisor. Moreover, it is unlikely that the employee will succeed in canvassing her colleagues' support against her supervisor, as they, too, were upset by her behaviour.

Sometimes it is necessary to create an opportunity to assert authority.

A newly-appointed hospital administrator found that her deputy resented working for a woman. He made it clear to other staff that he wasn't 'frightened of her', and that he proposed to operate as he pleased. His superior became aware of this and sought a means of emphasising her authority. She noticed that he never booked leave through her but submitted his card for retrospective confirmation. She sensed that this was deliberate and decided to use it against him.

On the next occasion, she quietly pointed out to her deputy that leave must be booked in advance and then kept a discreet watch on his diary. A few weeks later the deputy marked a day's leave again without seeking prior agreement. The administrator said nothing but sent a memo asking him to attend a meeting on the day that she knew he planned to be on holiday.

The deputy returned the papers with a note indicating that he would be off on that day. His superior saw him and asked, 'When did you arrange that with me?' After some discussion the deputy said he would book leave in future but insisted he would be 'off' that day.

The administrator's ploy had now succeeded. She immediately sent this confirmation to her deputy:

> I refer to our discussion this morning concerning your intention to take leave on Thursday. Despite my clear indication to you three weeks ago that all leave must be booked in advance through me, you had clearly planned to take the day off without consulting me. While I am of course prepared to assist if there is an emergency, I am not prepared to accept a statement that you will be 'off' that day. I need you to attend a meeting, and must reiterate what I said to you that if you absent yourself on Thursday without discussing the issue with me, I will regard you as absent without permission and you must be prepared to accept the consequences.

The deputy then registered a grievance. He claimed that the memo was threatening and demanded an apology. The district general manager who heard the case was unsympathetic. He concluded that there was nothing improper in the document or its contents. He accepted the administrator's argument that verbal communication had failed and the memo was a correct and proper attempt to alert the employee to the serious situation that was developing.

Note the careful phrasing of the memo: the administrator's willingness to consider leave in an emergency is deliberately included to give an impression of reasonableness. Similarly, quoting the deputy's words creates a contrasting impression of insolence and insubordination on his part. No particular form of disciplinary action is specified. Indeed, disciplinary action is not mentioned directly. Sufficient is said to warn the employee but his superior does not commit herself. Incidentally, had the deputy taken the day off, he could have been disciplined either for absence without permission or for disobedience.

Failure to carry out instructions

Kings have been defeated and the fate of nations changed by the failure of subordinates to comply with seemingly simple instructions. Often no deliberate disobedience is intended. Failures tend to reflect a combination of poor communication, conflicting priorities and inadequate supervision. Of these, the last is probably the most significant. It is insufficient to issue an instruction and then assume that it will be carried out. It is essential to check and re-check that orders are being executed in accordance with stipulated standards and timescales.

Where an employee consistently fails to deliver however, the best advice is to keep a record of:

- the instructions issued;

- the date of issue and timescale for completion;

- any reminders;

- whether, and to what extent instructions have been carried out; and

- the reasons for non-compliance.

Although it is not always practicable to issue written instructions, these are easier to pursue in a disciplinary context than verbal ones. Reminders, preferably written, are evidence of good management and emphasise the employee's tardiness. It is important to be able to show precisely the gap between requirements and delivery in a similar fashion to that outlined in Chapter Three on performance. Likewise, any reasons for non-compliance must be addressed so that they cannot continue to be used as excuses.

The employee who obeys to the letter

This is a tactic designed to frustrate management by perverse precision in carrying out instructions: 'Ah but,' says the employee, 'you didn't say I had to do that.' Since, however, the law expects employees to exercise common sense and judgement, this tactic can be countered on the basis of failure to exercise reasonable skill and care in the performance of duties. The more senior an employee, the more initiative may be expected from him. Equally, do not be put off by arguments such as 'You told me to use my judgement, and now you are criticising me'. You have a right to ascertain how judgement was exercised, and to pass comment on the quality of that judgement. For instance:

- Whom did the employee consult for advice?

- What other information did he seek?

- What factors did he take into account?

- What weight did he attach to these, and why?

- What risks were identified?

The next case shows how these questions can be applied in practice:

> A manager was faced with pickets on the factory gate. He called the police with the result that the unofficial stoppage escalated. The manager said he had been asking for guidance for months on how to deal with such a situation. As he had no support from senior management, he had used his initiative. He could not, he said, be blamed for doing so.

The chief executive, however, took a different view as the answers he received to the foregoing questions were negative. Consequently, the manager received a written warning which read:

Dear

On the day of the strike you failed to consult either personnel or your senior manager, who could have advised you on how to respond to the situation. I reject your assertion that you had received no written guidelines. No two stoppages are ever alike and therefore it is inappropriate and dangerous to issue rigid rules.

Your objective in calling the police appears to have been 'to show those buggers' as you put it. You did not take into account any other factors such as the very high probability of the conflict escalating, nor did you weigh this against the fact that the picket was a peaceful one. By your own admission, you had no grounds for believing there was any danger of unrest which might have warranted a police presence. At best, your actions were hasty and ill-considered; at worst they were motivated by vindictiveness. What is clear is that you failed to exercise the judgement and circumspection I would have expected from a senior manager.

Yours sincerely

Summary and checklist

- An employee is expected to obey his employer.

- Instructions must however:
  — be lawful;
  — not place the employee in danger;
  — be consistent with the scope of his responsibilities.

- An employee can be asked to undertake a task not specified in his job description, provided it is consistent with the general scope of his responsibilities.

- Never over-react to refusal. Sometimes it is best ignored.

- Apply power slowly. Keep your options open by deploying persuasive tactics first.

- Explore the reasons for non-compliance; often the real problem is hidden.

- Help the employee save face.

- Use the issue of an instruction as a tactic for signalling your authority.

- Deal with grievances in procedure before taking disciplinary action.

- Try and make un-cooperative employees feel valued. Stimulate commitment by creating excitement.

- Sometimes, a drastic counter-response is necessary to emphasise your authority.

- One tactic for dealing with negative employees is to force them onto the defensive.

- If disciplinary action becomes necessary, concentrate on issues where you have a strong case.

- Sometimes it is necessary to create an opportunity to exert your authority by deliberately allowing an employee to transgress.

- Keep a comprehensive written record of instructions issued and results obtained.

- An employee who obeys to the letter may be disciplined for failing to exercise skill and care.

Chapter Six
Other Forms of Serious Misconduct

Introduction

This chapter examines other forms of serious misconduct which may warrant dismissal for a first offence, depending upon the circumstances and gravity of the misdemeanour. This includes violence and intimidation; causing danger; unauthorised absence; drinking; and damage to property. A further category known as 'some other substantial reason' is covered in the next chapter.

Violence and intimidation

Fighting

Violence in the workplace is intolerable as it leads to gang warfare and sub-cultures based on threat. This is reflected in the fact that many organisations have strict rules whereby anyone involved in a fight is dismissed, regardless of who struck the first blow. However, while dismissal is potentially admissible, employers must be able to demonstrate that the decision was based upon a thorough investigation and proper weighing of evidence and other circumstances, regardless of what the rule book says.

Investigating violence

The investigation should cover the points set out in the following checklist.

Checklist for investigating violence

- Where and when did the fight start?

- How did it start?

- Was there provocation? If so, from whom, to what degree, and for how long?

- Have any of the participants been known to behave violently or aggressively?

- What happened during the fight?

- What level of force was used? Was it beyond the minimum required for self-defence?

- Were there any witnesses? If so, what do they say?

- If witnesses say they saw and heard nothing, is this likely, or does it suggest intimidation?

- Is the account of each participant consistent with injuries and other evidence?

The first step in investigating violence is to obtain an account of events leading up to the fight, and other background information, such as where and when the fight took place. In particular, was actual or potential danger created? If so, it adds significantly to the seriousness of the offence. Establish whether the incident was a spontaneous outburst or an accumulation of ill-feeling. The degree and extent of provocation may mitigate the disciplinary penalty. In particular, dismissal for a first offence may be unfair where there is intense and/or sustained provocation. Conversely, someone who provokes another employee may be guilty of serious misconduct, regardless of whether he uses physical violence himself. Similarly, evidence may weigh more heavily against someone who is habitually aggressive than against someone for whom violence is out of character.

Try and form a picture of what took place, blow by blow if possible. The level of force used by each person is a critical factor in validating participants' accounts and in deciding upon the disciplinary penalty. For example, evidence of repeated blows is inconsistent with an employee's claim to have lost his temper. The latter usually results in one spontaneous punch. Similarly, what level of force did the employee use to defend himself? Did he make any unnecessary physical contact. Were his posture and general gestures aggressive or defensive?

All witnesses should be interviewed, though some may prove reticent either as a result of loyalty or intimidation. If intimidation is suspected, it may be necessary to suspend one or both parties to facilitate an investigation. Even then, silence may still prevail. The best advice is to persist, because if one person begins to speak, others may follow. Where refusal to talk is suggestive of serious intimidation, this in itself may be sufficient evidence to justify dismissal.

Accounts of violence are often inconsistent. It is important to identify discrepancies within and between statements and deduce their implications in order to form reasoned conclusions. The following analysis of a case study illustrates what this means.

Analysing a case of violence

1. *Statement of First Employee: Pickles*

   The argument was still going on when I stopped the vehicle and Howard Jones reached over, grabbed the collar of my coat and pulled me forward. I tried to break away by putting my arm round Howard Jones' neck and telling him 'That's enough'. He then turned his body towards the driver's door and tried to get out of the vehicle. At this moment, Howard Jones pulled me backwards, causing me to fall backwards across the driver and passengers' seats on my back. Howard Jones held me on my back and struck several blows to my face. I tried to get out of this position by lifting my legs up and pushing him off with my feet, causing him to roll completely over and ending up outside of the vehicle.

2. *Statement of Second Employee: Jones*

   I was arguing with Tony Pickles and on arriving at Greentop Crescent, both of us were left in the vehicle. When Tony Pickles put his left arm round my neck and got me in an arm lock with my head low down, I dragged him backwards with my right arm and pushed him into the wall between the seats, which caused his injuries.

3. *Statement of Witness*

   The argument started when we were driving to the job. Mr Jones was blaming Mr Pickles for us being late. I saw a heated argument. Mr Jones stood pointing finger [sic] at Mr Pickles as if making a point. Mr Jones put [sic] arm round Mr Pickles' neck. Both operatives came out the passenger's door. Saw blood on Mr Pickles' face.

The injuries referred to in the second statement consisted of several cuts and bruises to Tony Pickles' eyes and face, requiring hospital treatment and stitching. Mr Jones did not report any injuries, though afterwards, an abrasion on the knuckle of his right hand was observed. He claimed to have sustained it moving flagstones later that morning. There were in fact several witnesses, all of whom gave similar accounts, except one who stated that he was at the door of the vehicle when the fight broke out, when his colleagues were emphatic that he was with them about 15 metres away. All witnesses said that Mr Jones was first to use force.

Are both employees guilty, or is one innocent? Is one more culpable than the other? Analysis reveals that:

- Regardless of who struck the first blow, there was a fight.

- Both parties used physical force beyond the minimum required for self-defence.

- There was provocation from Jones.

- Pickles' injuries are consistent with being struck several times.

What disciplinary penalty is appropriate? The most important point of the analysis is that both employees were unnecessarily violent. Jones' behaviour, however, was provocative and inappropriate for someone addressing his supervisor. Furthermore, the injuries received by Pickles are unlikely to have been caused by falling between the seats of the van, but are consistent with having been hit several times by Jones. Dismissal of both employees would probably be fair, in view of the level of violence. Jones was dismissed for being the most violent and most culpable. Pickles received a final warning.

Interestingly, it emerged after his dismissal that Jones, a former army sergeant, was known for aggression and bullying. On the morning before the fight, he pulled a young apprentice across a table and threatened him, a fact doubtless reflected in the tenor of the witnesses' statements.

Other forms of violence and assault

> Two care assistants were responsible for bathing an elderly and infirm man. They poured Dettol over his head and then left him sitting in tepid water for half an hour. They said it was meant as a joke.

Here, a vulnerable and dependent client has been deprived of his dignity and has been physically abused. Whatever the motive, the employees have clearly violated their position of trust. They were dismissed and did not appeal. The next case appears similarly serious but highlights the importance of carrying out a thorough investigation.

> A mother complained that the school nurse had ill-treated her daughter, who was sent for treatment following an ankle injury. She alleged that the nurse shouted at her daughter and plunged her foot into boiling water.
>
> The nurse denied the allegations. She stated that the only time she had raised her voice was when she was speaking on the telephone and the girl was trying to move. She spoke loudly and urgently to make herself heard and to prevent further injury. She had bathed the girl's ankle in hot water, the standard treatment for this type of injury.

Is the nurse a Dickensian ogre or is there some other explanation? The investigation revealed that another boy was in the first-aid room at the same time as the girl. He confirmed that the room was very noisy that day, and that the nurse did break off her telephone conversation to tell the girl to keep still. The boy was quite clear that the nurse did not shout, nor did she sound angry. He saw the ankle bathed and said that the girl did not complain about the temperature of the water.

Had the investigator been less patient and thorough, the presence of a witness might not have emerged or been followed up. Finally, the headteacher was interviewed. He said that the nurse had been praised for her care and compassion. He then added that the girl's mother had been an unsuccessful applicant for the post.

Intimidation

Intimidation is as serious as fighting because the consequences are identical, but it is less visible. Detection, therefore, requires vigilance. Some of the signs are:

- a sudden deterioration in morale, or sudden uplift;
- deference paid to one or a small group of employees;
- veiled hints of corruption or sinister undercurrents amongst employees;
- cash exchanging hands in or outside the workplace.

The implications of a sudden deterioration in morale are obvious. An upsurge is also significant — it may mean that the aggressor has gone on holiday. Deference is a sign of fear. It is important to be alert to oblique indications that staff are being coerced. Trade union officials are worth probing as they are often attuned to undercurrents in the workplace. Money changing hands is extremely suspicious, especially if there are other indications of malaise. Is there a protection racket afoot or other organised workplace crime? Airport baggage handlers, for example, have been known to perpetuate theft by planting money in the lockers of newcomers. Those who accept the cash become identified with iniquity, those who decline find their working lives made intolerable.*

The covert nature of intimidation and consequent fear makes evidence difficult to obtain. Employees practising coercion, however, are quite likely to commit other forms of serious misconduct. Miscreants should therefore be quietly observed. If possible, focus upon offences where reliance on witnesses is minimal.

Mental intimidation

Intimidation may be mental as well as physical:

A 16-year-old office clerk became infatuated with a salesman. Her attentions were rejected and so she made a series of anonymous telephone calls to the salesman's wife, alleging that he was having an affair with someone.

The wife was extremely distressed. Details of the conversation led her to suspect someone from her husband's work. Moreover, at the time of one of the calls, the girl was seen by another member of staff replacing a telephone receiver and saying to her friend 'That's it, she's crying now'.

The employee's denials were rejected on the balance of probabilities. She received a final warning for her 'spiteful and selfish behaviour' which had distressed both the salesman and his wife and had strained their marriage. Had she been older, the warning said, she would have been dismissed. The friend received a written warning.

* Moynahan, B (1978) *Airport International* Pan Books, London.

> Graham, one of my staff, came to my house on Sunday afternoon. He had been drinking and said he wanted us to let bygones be bygones. I said I would see him in the office on Monday. He said 'OK, Jim, you're the boss, but just remember, I've got you taped', by which I understood him to mean he was trying to blackmail me.

The word 'taped' in this statement refers to a recording made by the employee of a conversation between him and his supervisor, and which he told other staff he had made. At the disciplinary hearing, the employee claimed that the tape was intended to remind his supervisor of a commitment to order materials. It was pointed out, however, that there was no evidence of his using it for this purpose. The employee received a final warning for trying to intimidate his supervisor.

Violence and intimidation outside work

Conduct outside work is covered in detail in the following chapter. Essentially, violence and intimidation which occur outside work are a legitimate managerial concern if they impact upon the efficacy of the organisation. In my experience, physical violence is by no means unknown, especially, though not exclusively, among blue-collar workers. Indeed, in some organisations, it is a tacitly accepted means of resolving workplace issues. Such violence tends to take place either in quiet places on site, or after work. The best advice for managers and personnel officers is to create a climate whereby it is made clear that violence is unacceptable. Moreover, all reports should be investigated, and action taken where appropriate as a major reason for the perpetuation of violence is the workforce's belief that no one is prepared to do anything about it.

Causing danger

Managing safety

Accidents do not simply happen. They are caused. The likelihood of sanctions does little to prevent accidents. Employees must be trained in safe working practices and be encouraged to 'think safety'. Many accidents are caused by carelessness, ranging from a momentary lapse of concentration to wholesale neglect, often through taking shortcuts. Training and reward systems should, therefore, be conducive to safe working practices. Safety should be taken into account when designing incentive schemes, tendering for work and specifying performance standards. Safety clothing and equipment should be user-friendly.

That said, causing danger, wilfully or inadvertently, is a serious disciplinary offence because of the potentially catastrophic consequences. Like all disciplinary matters, the penalty depends upon the circumstances. Someone walking through a depot loaded with highly inflammable cylinders, absently smoking a cigarette, is causing danger but differs from someone recklessly driving a van along a pavement in a city centre to dodge a traffic queue. The former is behaving absentmindedly; the latter, with wilful disregard.

Investigating accidents

An important function of an accident investigation is to prevent a recurrence. Enquiries should therefore be broad based. Technical and organisational factors as well as human failings should be examined. The following checklist may be useful.

Checklist for investigating accidents

- Was the danger caused wilfully or by carelessness?

- If carelessness was the cause, what was the degree of carelessness?

- Should the employee have known that his actions were dangerous?

- What training has he received?

- Did anything prevent the employee from working safely?

- Are working practices conducive to safety?

- What safety devices are available? Were they used, and how effective are they?

- What other factors might have played a part, for example: stress and fatigue; equipment in poor working order; time pressures; imprecise instructions?

- In general, how much managerial attention is devoted to safety?

- What must be done to prevent a recurrence?

We now examine the implications of the key points on the checklist.

The importance of training

It is dangerous to assume that employees are safety conscious, even at the most basic level, as the example below demonstrates.

The supervisor of part of a youth training workshop was disciplined for allowing planks of wood to be stacked in front of a door marked 'Fire Exit'. Management's case was that the supervisor had been negligent. He should have seen the danger and done something about it.

The trade union representative took a different view. Replying to management's point about the notice, he said 'I accept that my member can read, but when was he sent on a safety awareness course? He is a temporary employee whose previous experience was in an office. How could you expect him to appreciate the hazards in a workshop? The wood had been there for weeks. Why didn't the workshop manager notice it and do something? It seems that he is scapegoating my member to detract from his own negligence.

The purpose of training is to create and emphasise safety awareness. In addition, access to procedures and information required for safe working should be readily available. Safety regulations should be:

- clear;

- comprehensive;

- readily accessible; and

- emphatic.

The next case illustrates the importance of these points.

A kitchen supervisor allowed a consignment of chicken to be stored alongside some cooked ham in a refrigerator. The ham became contaminated with salmonella bacteria from the raw chicken, resulting in an outbreak of food poisoning.

The enquiry found that food hygiene rules were contained in a small, clearly written, easy-to-follow handbook which was even illustrated with cartoons to maximise its readability. The handbook was issued to all staff and emphatically stated that cooked and uncooked meats must never, under any circumstances, be stored together. Separate fridges were provided for this purpose. The supervisor denied storing the two meats in the same fridge but his explanation was rejected as laboratory analysis found traces of both meats in the same vicinity. He was, therefore, dismissed.

Is the employee really to blame?

Many readers will be familiar with the tale of the amateur railway driver during the General Strike. An inspector observed that the pressure gauge was rather low. 'Oh that,' replied the driver 'it's on its second time around.' The moral of this story is that unsafe working practices or equipment will sooner or later cause an accident, no matter how careful the employee. For example:

> A deep-fat fryer was left switched on in a school kitchen overnight. The entire school, only recently opened, burned to the ground. The head cook could not explain how it had happened as she was certain that the fryer had been switched off.

Was the head cook negligent or was there some other explanation? This case shows the importance of carrying out a comprehensive investigation and not simply seeking to apportion blame. Tests carried out with an identical model showed that the dial on the fryer was such that when turned to the 'off' position, it could still be on. In other words, the real cause of the accident was a poorly designed switch.

Safety and health

If, in your judgement, an employee's state of health makes him a potential danger:

- remove him from the workplace immediately; and
- obtain medical advice.

For example:

> A cook returned to work after a heart attack. Although she insisted that she was fit, to her manager she appeared 'shaky'. The job involved handling pans of boiling water and a great deal of bending and heavy lifting. The manager felt that she was a potential danger yet did not know what to do because the cook's own doctor had declared her fit to return to work.

Where even the slightest grounds exist for believing that an employee is a danger, you must act. Here, the fact that the cook's doctor has permitted her to return to work is irrelevant. He is not there to see her in action. Besides, he may not appreciate what the cook's job involves and she might have indicated that she was fitter than she actually felt, just to get back to work, especially if her sick pay entitlement had expired. This is why independent medical advice is essential.

If necessary, an employee can be instructed to leave. Usually though, given a little understanding and patience, most employees will accede, gladly perhaps. Some people feel guilty about being absent and would rather someone else made the decision. There are exceptions however:

A labourer returned to work after a shoulder injury. He proved capable of only light duties, however, and admitted that his doctor had certified him fit only under duress. The labourer said that he would cooperate if his manager suspended him, but he refused to obtain a sick note from his own doctor.

Medical suspension is normally with full pay unless the contract of employment states otherwise. The labourer's sick pay entitlement had expired and this was a ploy to extend payment. In this situation, the manager can instruct the employee to see his doctor or, if he refuses, can suspend him pending a disciplinary hearing for disobedience.

An employee's responsibility for his own health

Employees are expected to take reasonable care of their health.

An art gallery attendant who was epileptic suffered a number of seizures. He would appear vacant for a minute or so and sometimes lost consciousness momentarily. Management were concerned that he might collapse while working on a ladder or while in some other dangerous position.

In truth, management were more concerned about potential damage to a picture than about damage to the employee. An independent medical report indicated tht the employee's epilepsy was controllable by drugs. The attacks resulted from drinking and meddling with the dosage. The employee was therefore told, sympathetically but firmly, that he must follow medical advice. Had he disregarded this instruction, he could legitimately have been warned and could even have been dismissed eventually.

Unauthorised absence

Legal principles

In law, an employee is expected to report for work every day unless sick or specifically granted leave. Absence without permission may be either repudiation or misconduct. The former applies where the employee indicates by his behaviour that he does not intend to be bound by the contract. The latter occurs where the evidence suggests that the employee is generally willing to be bound but has committed a breach, such as failing to submit sick notes. Although both of these are serious, it is important not to over-react but to investigate, and to give the employee a chance to explain.

Dealing with an employee who disappears

First make reasonable enquiries as to the employee's whereabouts as follows.

Checklist for investigating where an employee is absent without permission

- If practicable, ask colleagues if they know of the employee's whereabouts, and of anything preventing him from reporting for work.

- Write to the employee at his last known address.

- In the letter, explain that he is absent without permission and must get in touch with you.

- If possible, hand deliver the letter.

- Even if the house appears unoccupied or the employee has moved away, try to deliver the letter, as he may return.

- If the employee has moved away, try and obtain his new address.

- After a fortnight, write again.

- This time, point out that your previous letter has gone unanswered, and that if you do not hear from him within a stipulated period (two weeks is normally reasonable), you will assume that he has repudiated his contract.

Similar principles apply where an employee fails to take up an offer of employment, except that it is sufficient to write only once or twice at the most. In practice, few employees ever respond. Nevertheless, avoid sounding officious or threatening. I once received a reply from someone's daughter, apologising for the length of time taken to respond and informing me that her mother, the employee, was dead.

Unauthorised absence

There is a difference between an employee who disappears without any intention of returning to work and someone who violates the contract, for example, by failing to submit sick notes or by disregarding his employer's instructions. The steps outlined in the checklist should be followed but absence is most safely treated as a disciplinary matter rather than as repudiation. For example:

Mr Sykes was counselled in May by his manager following 170 days sickness in one year. In August, he was twice absent again but failed to submit sick notes. A personnel officer visited and Mr Sykes drove off in his car as he saw him approach. The personnel officer left a note instructing Mr Sykes to attend a meeting to discuss his unauthorised absence. He did not do so and a second visit was made. This time Mr Sykes was out. Again he failed to attend a meeting, as required in another note posted through his door.

A letter was then sent to Mr Sykes requiring him for the third time to attend a meeting to discuss his absence. The letter stated: 'Failure to attend this meeting will lead to your employment being terminated [sic] for not attending the meeting and for the following reasons . . . .' (The reasons being failure to attend previous meetings and non-submission of sick notes.)

Mr Sykes telephoned the company on the morning of the meeting to say that he had problems with his car. The meeting was, therefore, rearranged. Mr Sykes, however, again failed to appear and another letter was sent saying 'Your employment has been terminated with immediate effect'.

Mr Sykes' trade union threatened industrial action unless the letter was withdrawn. What management should have done was to write to Mr Sykes again, this time instructing him to attend a disciplinary hearing to explain himself. Had he then failed to appear, they could have dismissed him, or, better still, could have given him one last opportunity by calling a further hearing. Mr Sykes' dismissal was unfair as he had been deprived of an opportunity to explain that his doctor had misdirected his sick notes, and that severe personal problems had affected his behaviour.

Whether or not the hearing would have accepted these explanations is irrelevant. The point is that the employee was deprived of the opportunity to present them.

Ironically, trade union intervention saved the case. The letter was withdrawn and Mr Sykes was suspended pending a disciplinary hearing, where he was dismissed. Had he accepted his initial dismissal, an industrial tribunal would have probably found it unfair, albeit that he contributed to it.

Overstaying leave

Many organisations require employees taking extended leave to sign a paper accepting dismissal if they fail to return by the stipulated date. In fact, rigid enforcement of such a document would probably be unfair. The ACAS Guide urges employers to investigate in the normal way, and to behave reasonably. Terms and conditions under which leave is granted should be explained and the employee's signature obtained as confirmation that he understands them. Where an employee fails to return by the agreed date, reasonable enquiries as to his whereabouts should be made. Employers should bear in mind that it may take several weeks for sick notes to arrive from abroad and avoid treating these in a discriminatory fashion because they happen to be foreign. Any decision to dismiss should take into account the employee's record and service.

Drinking

Drinking can be dangerous. For this reason, many organisations have strict rules forbidding alcohol consumption both on duty, and at certain off duty times. Employees may even be forbidden to bring alcohol on to the premises and be dismissed if they contravene this rule. Providing rules are demonstrably necessary and well-publicised, industrial tribunals will uphold their enforcement even though the consequences seem harsh. For example, dismissal for bringing a bottle of whisky aboard an oil rig was judged fair, even though the act was inadvertent, and the bottle had not been opened. The tribunal accepted that the rule was so critical to safety that no exception could be mde. Even where no rule exists, dismissal may be fair if it can be shown that the employee ought to have known that he was likely to cause danger. Where an employee appears to be under the influence of alcohol and therefore a safety risk, he should be sent home.

Distinguishing alcoholism from drinking

An employee's work may suffer as a consequence of alcoholism, yet he may never actually drink at work. Someone who happens to be drunk on duty however is not necessarily an alcoholic. Alcohol-dependence should be dealt with by counselling rather than by discipline. For example:

> A classroom assistant regularly reported for work smelling of whisky. Staff noticed that her speech was often slurred and that she regularly disappeared for periods of up to 40 minutes. She was dreamy and inefficient, and the children had little respect for her.

Investigations revealed that this was not a disciplinary case. The employee had severe family problems. Her husband was suffering from cancer and her daughter and children had moved in with her following the break up of the daughter's marriage.

Damage to property

The law expects an employee to take reasonable care of his employer's property and of property belonging to other employees. Wilful damage such as industrial sabotage, including corruption of computer software, constitutes gross misconduct.

> An engineer's mate placed a leather glove inside the workings of a computerised weaving loom, causing several thousands of pounds worth of damage and disrupting production for a fortnight.

Damage here was quite intentional and therefore dismissal was justified. Accidental damage should generally be regarded more leniently, depending upon the degree of carelessness. For instance:

> A gang of workmen parked their pick-up truck near a cafe. When they emerged from their tea break, they were horrified to discover that spades and other equipment loaded onto the truck had vanished.

Although the loss was accidental, nevertheless the equipment should not have been left unattended. Each employee, therefore, received a first warning for carelessness.

The spirit in which damage occurs is more important than the extent of the calamity in deciding whether trust is destroyed.

A deaf and dumb employee was fascinated by vehicles. One Friday night, he broke into the depot and drove off in a company van. Despite the fact that he had no driving licence, he drove all over the city, until the van ran out of fuel, whereupon he abandoned it. The vehicle was subsequently recovered minus its wheels.

Although the damage to property was significant, unlike the case of the glove, the employee was motivated not by malice, but by a personal obsession. Indeed, no one could bring themselves to sack him. Instead a final warning was issued. The offence was not repeated.

Is an employee's illness genuine?

Many managers and personnel officers have observed the ease with which sick notes can be obtained. It is seldom profitable to argue that an employee's illness is feigned but better to concentrate upon the fact that an employee is either:

- breaching his contract; or

- retarding his recovery.

In both cases employers are normally expected to counsel and warn employees first. Dismissal may be admissible, however, where a serious breach of contract is committed, as in the following case.

A labourer submitted sick notes to cover a fortnight's absence from work because of back strain. It was subsequently discovered however that he had undertaken community service during this period.

The employee argued that he was unfit to carry out his normal duties but able to undertake community service which involved only light work. The employer refused to accept this explanation and dismissed the employee. Similarly:

A tradesman absent for four months with a knee injury was anonymously reported to be working for another firm. His manager mounted surveillance and observed the employee getting into a van parked outside his home at 7.30 am every day for a fortnight. The employee was dressed in working clothes and carried a tool kit. The manager followed the van on each occasion but invariably lost sight of it when the city was reached 15 miles away.

One morning the employee was challenged as he approached the van. He said he had been visiting his mother who was ill. This was rejected as his mother lived in the opposite direction to that taken by the van.

The investigation here has been sufficiently thorough to conclude, on the balance of probabilities, that the employee was working either for himself, or for someone else in his employer's time. Consequently he was dismissed.

Retarding recovery

A common defence of employees is that work or exercise is conducive to recovery. It is therefore advisable to obtain medical evidence, as was done in the following instance, before taking disciplinary action.

An employee suffering from groin strain was challenged by his manager who found him playing golf. The employee maintained his strain did not impede him. He had become depressed at home and exercise helped relieve this.

Management in fact suspected that the employee's injury was far from serious. A medical report unequivocally stated that a groin injury would be aggravated by playing golf. The employee therefore received a written warning for retarding his recovery.

Employee refused leave and subsequently reports sick

This is a familiar problem to many managers and personnel officers. Indeed, some organisations emphasise their willingness to grant leave at short notice for emergencies knowing that the alternative is to lose a day's production through sickness absence. In principle, however, employers are entitled to require leave to be arranged in advance. Employers are further entitled to discipline employees who commit misconduct by reporting sick when refused leave. The strongest guide to probabilities in these circumstances is the employee's previous conduct and whether he has declared his intentions in advance. The next case is an unusual variation on a theme.

An employee's request for leave was refused on grounds of insufficient notice. The employee then declared that he would take the time off as sick leave. This he duly did. He subsequently claimed that the balance of his mind had been disturbed, and that this had affected his behaviour.

The employee in fact had a history of anxiety and depression plus a previous warning for refusing to obey an instruction and for aggressive behaviour. He was, moreover, due to face a charge of grievous bodily harm. A psychiatric examination was arranged partly to satisfy the trade union and partly to check whether the man's history of aggression meant that he could be a danger to others. The report indicated that the employee was suffering from 'paranoia experienced in 80 per cent of the population'. This, the doctor explained, meant there was nothing wrong with the man.

Summary and checklist

- Gross misconduct may also include violence and intimidation; causing danger; unauthorised absence; drinking; and damage to property.

- Dismissal must reflect a proper investigation and weighing of the circumstances. Rigid enforcement of rules is unfair unless these preconditions are satisfied.

- The critical factors in deciding whether to dismiss someone for fighting are:
  — whether danger was caused;
  — the degree and extent of provocation;
  — the level of force used.

- Intimidation may be mental as well as physical.

- Accidents do not happen, they are caused.

- Staff should be trained to 'think safety'.

- No matter how careful the employee, unsafe equipment or working practices will inevitably lead to an accident.

- Where even the slightest possibility exists that an employee's health makes him a danger, he should be sent home and independent medical advice obtained.

- Where an employee disappears or fails to take up an offer of employment, reasonable efforts should be made to contact him before concluding he has repudiated his contract.

- Where an employee is absent without permission but has not gone away, it may be safer to treat the problem as a disciplinary one.

- Automatic dismissal for overstaying leave may be unfair, even if the employee has signed an undertaking accepting it.

- Tribunals will uphold strict rules concerning alcohol, providing they can be shown to be necessary.

- Wilful damage to property is tantamount to gross misconduct.

- Violation of trust is more significant than the extent of the damage.

- It is seldom profitable to suggest that an employee's illness is feigned. It is better to concentrate upon a possible breach of contract or retardation of recovery.

Chapter Seven
Dismissal for 'Some Other Substantial Reason'

Introduction

This book has so far been concerned with capability and conduct. Dismissal is also admissible for what is known as 'Some other substantial reason; (SOSR). SOSR may be defined as anything sufficiently serious in an employer's eyes to warrant dismissal. Seriousness depends upon:

- the culture, and norms of the organisation;

- the employee's role;

- operational exigencies;

- whether trust and confidence in the employee has been destroyed.

Standards of conduct reflect the culture and norms of the organisation. Absenteeism, for example, is generally viewed seriously. In the case of the abattoir cited on page 49, however, the slaughtermen are renowned for hard drinking and brawling. Consequently, the manager's first task on a Monday morning is to telephone local police stations to check how many men have been locked up over the weekend! If he sacked everyone guilty of habitual absence he would be left with an extremely depleted workforce. Similarly, swearing at a supervisor would be unacceptable in many organisations yet unremarkable, say, on a building site.

An employee's role is also significant. For instance, a factory operative convicted of a sexual offence might not present a problem to his employer, whereas someone working with young children or other vulnerable groups certainly would.

On the third point, operational necessity may leave an employer with no alternative but to dismiss; for example, if he must engage a permanent replacement for an employee sent to prison.

We have seen in previous chapters how trust can be violated through dishonesty, for example. This chapter examines how other forms of behaviour such as divulgence of trade secrets or conduct outside work can destroy an employer's confidence in an employee.

The possibilities of dismissal for SOSR are extremely wide. It is hoped, however, that the examples which follow are sufficiently comprehensive at least to facilitate insight into what dismissal for 'Some other substantial reason', means in practice.

Imprisonment

The legal background

> A porter received a six-month jail sentence for a Social Security fraud. The job of a porter was being phased out and his employers did nothing. Then, one morning, his sentence served, the porter reported for work.

An employee who is imprisoned, remanded in custody or prevented from working normally because of bail conditions, does not automatically lose his job. However, once it is clear that someone's continued employment is impracticable, dismissal for SOSR may be fair; or the contract may be frustrated.

The doctrine of frustration was originally applied to commercial transactions and only recently to employment contracts. Basically, frustration occurs when, through neither party's fault, an unforeseen event prevents performance of the contract as originally envisaged.

Imprisonment: employer's responsibilities

No definitive rules exist on when a contract becomes frustrated, or when an employer is entitled to dismiss. This depends upon:

- how long the employer can cope without the employee's services;
- whether it is essential to engage a permanent replacement;
- the likely length of the employee's absence; and
- the reason for an employee's absence.

A conviction for murder, say, or a long custodial sentence will almost certainly frustrate the contract. A very short period of absence, however, would not — unless it is essential to employ a permanent replacement immediately. As a guide, employers are expected to wait for as long as they would allow someone to be absent due to sickness.

Employers are required to behave reasonably in deciding whether to keep an employee's job open. Reasonable in this context means taking into account the employee's length of service and work record as well as the expected length of absence. Other pertinent factors include whether the employee has maintained contact and whether he could have prevented imprisonment by paying a fine, for example.

Employers are further expected to make reasonable enquiries from the employee's family and solicitor about the nature of the charge, trial date and the likelihood of an appeal before making a decision. It is advisable to request information in writing partly because it assists the solicitor in obtaining his client's cooperation, but more particularly because the copy letter is proof of an attempt to investigate. A specimen draft is set out below:

> Dear
>
> I understand that you are acting for George Smith. Mr Smith has been absent from work since —— My information is that he is being detained on remand at —— charged with —— Please would you confirm this and the date of Mr Smith's trial.
>
> Yours sincerely

Dismissal or frustration?

Where the reason for an employee's detention destroys trust or reflects adversely upon his employer, dismissal for SOSR may be appropriate even where the length of the sentence would in any case frustrate the contract. For instance:

A painter employed by a housing charity returned to an aged person's residence, where he had been working, with the intention of robbing her. The painter was disturbed by the old lady whom he then murdered with a pair of scissors.

It is stressed, however, that dismissal upon sentencing is not automatically admissible. Each case must be considered on its merits.

An electrical inspector whose job entailed working in homes received four months' imprisonment for receiving stolen goods. While it was feasible to keep his job open, the manager wanted to dismiss the inspector as he no longer trusted him to work in customers' homes.

The safest strategy here is to notify the employee that his job will be kept open, but, because of the nature of the offence, a disciplinary enquiry will be held upon his release which may result in dismissal. This gives the employee an opportunity to state his case and for alternative options such as transfer to another post to be considered. Perfunctory dismissal on the other hand would probably be unfair as there is no pressing need to engage a replacement.

Severing the contract

The advantage of declaring a contract frustrated is that there is, by definition, no dismissal. No action is required, the contract simply lapses and both parties' obligations cease. However, it is courtesy to write to the employee notifying him that because of his imprisonment, his contract has ended 'by operation of law'. Correspondence is best addressed to the employee's solicitor.

It is emphasised that a record of convictions is essential and that prospective employee's are checked against it. It is surprising how quickly staff move on and ex-employees may reapply and conceal their previous employment or how it ended.

Sexual harassment

The legal significance of sexual harassment

Although not explicitly forbidden by statute, sexual harassment is unlawful because it is tantamount to detrimental treatment on grounds of gender under the Sex Discrimination Act 1975. The term sexual harassment is actually a misnomer because unlawful conduct:

- need not be an attempt to embark upon sexual relations; nor

- be continuous.

A single serious incident can amount to detrimental treatment. For disciplinary purposes, it is best to focus upon misconduct rather than be distracted by arguments over definitions. However, it is emphasised that allegations of sexual harassment must be taken seriously. This means employers must:

- investigate complaints properly; and

- if substantiated, take appropriate action against those responsible.

Failure to do so can result in a finding of sex discrimination and a finding of constructive dismissal. For example:

Mr Daly put the light out, Mr Smith picked up her legs and put them round him . . . Mr Daly . . . put his hands between her legs and touched her private parts remarking 'You've got a big one'. She was eventually able to open the door and run out. After shouting that she was going to report the incident they replied it would be her word against theirs.

. . . she made a complaint to Miss Renolds [who] made some enquiry and decided, in the light of denials from both Mr Smith and Mr Daly, that no steps should be taken. Mrs Darby [the employee] left a week later saying . . . that if she was to be treated in this way she could not really feel she was obtaining justice at a proper inquiry and she therefore felt that she had been constructively dismissed. (*Bracebridge Engineering Ltd* v *Darby*, IRLR, (3), 1990.)

Those hearing the case concurred.

Investigating sexual harassment

I entered the locker room and saw the caretaker standing by the window. He had his back to me and I noticed that he seemed to be shaking. Then he turned round and I saw that his penis was exposed. He didn't say anything and I ran out of the room. I went to the toilet and was sick.

Complainants of sexual harassment often suffer distress and embarrassment. Investigations must therefore be conducted with sensitivity. It is advisable to:

- provide someone of the same sex as investigating officer;

- invite the complainant to be interviewed in the presence of a friend or trade union official;

- assure and, if necessary, reassure the complainant that the incident is being taken seriously.

Common strategies for defending accusations of sexual harassment are either to minimise the facts, and/or to suggest that the complainant misinterpreted the other person's behaviour. It is critical, therefore, to establish exactly what took place in addition to ascertaining:

- what was said;

- what the complainant understood the other person to mean;
- how the complainant felt about what happened;
- whether physical contact occurred.

The importance of covering these points is illustrated by the next case.

> A school teacher visited a historic monument with a group of children. The attendant who met the party stared at a badge upon her chest and said 'That's a nice badge'. During the trip he asked some of the children whether the teacher was married or if she had a boy friend. While the children were working on an exercise he came up and sat next to her on the stairs. His breath smelt of beer and he tried to hold her hand on the pretext of looking at her rings.

Before reading the next paragraph, ask yourself, how would you defend the attendant?

> In fact, the attendant's trade union representative suggested that the teacher had over-reacted to the exchange over the badges. He said that the attendant collected badges and was genuinely interested in the teacher's which was unusual. The questions concerning her marital status were just light-hearted banter with the children. The visit had taken place on a Friday when it was the attendant's custom to treat himself to a pub lunch with half a pint of bitter. Aware of the need to maintain good customer relations he had tried to be friendly and keep the teacher company while she was unoccupied. Her rings were striking and he had simply wanted a closer look at them.

The trade union representative here is seeking both to minimise the incident, and to suggest that the complainant has misinterpreted the attendant's behaviour.

However, the evidence is sufficiently detailed to withstand attack, in that analysis reveals three substantive concerns, namely:

1. The initial exchange concerning the badge
2. The questions about the teacher's marital status.
3. The attendant's behaviour on the stairs.

The first of these is indeed open to interpretation. However, taken in context with what followed, on balance the teacher's perceptions are probably well founded. The questions pertaining to marital status were inappropriate and should not have been asked. Furthermore, the attendant had no need to seat himself where he did. This alone was overly familiar behaviour towards a member of the public. Although the trade union representative glosses over it, there is no dispute that physical contact occurred. This too was inappropriate. Altogether then, it is possible to identify a basis for disciplinary action.

An employer's obligation to investigate allegations of sexual harassment by no means implies unquestioning acceptance of the complainant's account. As with all disciplinary investigations, an open mind is essential as the next case shows.

A woman alleged that an electrician sent to carry out repairs in her flat had tried to persuade her to have sexual intercourse. She said that the electrician had been very familiar, had made suggestive remarks, tried to fondle her and had given her money.

The electrician denied the allegation. He admitted that he had been friendly and laughed and joked with the woman about 'brewing up' and so forth. He noticed that the woman was living in poverty and because he had felt sorry for her, had given her £1.50 (which was all the cash he carried), to buy chips for her children.

Is the allegation malicious, or is it that there is no smoke without fire? The complainant was told that the electrician's manager would call to investigate. On reflection, however, it was decided to send a female personnel officer. The complainant (expecting a man), answered the door wearing a 'see-through nightdress'. Her response to the news that the electrician had been suspended was 'Oh I don't want him sacked, I've written him a Christmas card'. Her account was confused and she openly admitted that she was a heroin user.

Obviously no one will ever know exactly what happened though clearly the reliability of the complainant's evidence is questionable and insufficient grounds upon which to base a belief that misconduct took place.

Employee competition and confidentiality

Legal principles

An employee's duty to provide loyal, faithful and honest service forbids him to:

- compete with his employer;

- make secret profits from his employment; and

- divulge confidential information or trade secrets.

This duty further implies that an employee must devote all his working hours to his employment. A breach of any of these duties is tantamount to misconduct and if it results in the employer's trust being destroyed, he is entitled to dismiss, regardless of the actual damage caused.

Employee competing with employer

Competing with an employer, including soliciting his customers either directly or for a third party, is a dismissable offence. Dismissal simply because of an intention to compete, however, is unfair as the employee may not realise his plans are incompatible with his employment and be willing to drop them. It is essential, therefore, to discuss the issue with the employee before making any decision.

Seeking employment with a competitor, or giving notice to work for one, can justify dismissal if an abuse of position or confidentiality is entailed. Similarly, demanding unreasonable terms and conditions as an alternative to working for a competitor is a dismissable offence if the employer's trust is destroyed.

Making of secret profits by an employee

Secret profits can be defined as any financial benefit accruing to an employee as a result of his employment without his employer's knowledge or approval. This includes gifts, though dismissal would probably be found unfair if their value was small — such as a key ring or a diary — or if the benefits were not appropriated personally by the employee, as described below.

> The head of a purchasing department was suspended after it was revealed that suppliers' representatives were charged £50 for an appointment. Proceedings were dropped when it emerged that this was standard practice throughout the organisation and that all monies had been donated to staff funds.

Although in this case no secret profit accrued to the employee, practices such as this are undesirable as they can lead to corruption. Organisations are therefore urged to adopt codes of probity, specifying for example:

- What gifts may be accepted.

- A procedure for disposal of gifts which employees are forbidden to keep but which it would seem churlish to return.

- What level of hospitality may be offered.

- What level of hospitality may be accepted.

- Rules concerning solicitation of gifts.

- Reporting procedures if a bribe is offered.

Although these rules may seem primarily applicable to public service organisations, it should be remembered that private companies stand to lose incalculable amounts through being over-charged as a result of employees receiving secret commissions. Security-conscious management is also important as opportunities for abuse are invariably exploited. For example:

> For safety reasons an oil company replaced all light bulbs on oil rigs periodically, regardless of whether they had expired. These subsequently turned up on a market stall. The employee who supplied the stall holder denied behaving dishonestly. He said that when he had asked what to do with the bulbs he was told to use his initiative. The bulbs were removed from the shore openly in full view of management who, in two years, never queried their disposal.

Procedures alone, however, are inadequate. They must be properly enforced, as this case testifies.

> A building company ordered £800,000 worth of timber to make into windowframes. The price of timber is based upon quality. The supply ordered had a life expectancy of 10 to 15 years, though in appearance it would be identical to wood with a life expectancy of only five years. The only means of identifying the quality was through a trade stamp on each block.
>
> After six years all the frames manufactured from that consignment had rotted. An investigation found that the wood had been processed and the frames installed without the timber first having been inspected by stores staff.

The implication here is that the production manager had secretly arranged for a delivery of inferior wood and had probably shared the difference in price with someone from the suppliers. The manufacturing company were sued for heavy damages which could have been prevented if proper stores procedures had been enforced.

Disclosure of confidential information

This is a potentially dismissable offence depending on:

- The nature of the information.

- Whether disclosure was accidental or deliberate.

- Whether the employee was motivated by gain.

- The employee's role within the organisation.

Generally speaking, disclosure of financial or trade secrets for gain will almost certainly be a dismissable offence. The principle of fidelity, however, applies to all information.

> A trainee clerk told everyone he met that the chief accountant had been sacked. He knew this because he had seen the dismissal letter on the director's desk.

Obviously the letter should not have been left on the desk. However the director was about to sign it when he was interrupted. Besides, the document was marked 'private and confidential', and therefore the employee should have known his conduct was reprehensible. Conversely, although disclosure was deliberate, it was not for gain. Moreover the clerk was a low-ranking and inexperienced employee. Had he been the director's secretary for example, disclosure would have resulted in more serious disciplinary action than a first warning.

An employer is also entitled to protect himself from potential disclosure of confidential information. For example, an employee whose spouse goes to work for a rival firm may be fairly dismissed if there is a genuine possibility that the employer may be significantly harmed as a result.

Conduct outside the workplace

Legal principles

In law, an employee's conduct outside work is his own business provided it does not:

- conflict with his role within the organisation; or
- reflect adversely upon his employer; or
- otherwise harm the employer.

We now examine some of the ways in which an employee's private life can conflict with his contractual obligations.

Second employment

A second employment outside working hours is permissible provided it does not:

- significantly harm the employer;
- affect the employee's ability to devote full attention and effort to his job; or
- contravene any express rule forbidding it.

A principal careers officer discovered that an employment assistant had set up a private employment agency. He was concerned because of the employee's access to resources and confidential details of clients.

Although there was a rule whereby senior staff were required to seek permission before taking up outside employment, juniors, including the employment assistant, were excluded. The manager therefore felt powerless.

Junior staff's exemption from the rules concerning second employment is irrelevant because in law, the basic duty of fidelity applies to all employees. Here the employer has identified a valid conflict of interest. The employee then offered various guarantees of probity which were rightly declined as they were incapable of resolving the potential for abuse which was intolerable to the employer.

The employee subsequently agreed to withdraw from the agency. Had he refused, it would have been necessary formally to warn him against continuing, and, if this failed, to have eventually dismissed him.

Unpaid activities

Although no clear and definite rules exist on this topic, it seems reasonable to suggest that unpaid activities may be legitimate grounds for concern if they impinge upon a person's employment. Active membership of certain political parties or pressure groups, for example, may be inconsistent with an employee's role within the organisation. It would be unacceptable for someone employed as a coordinator of a lesbian and gays' support centre to join the National Front. Likewise, it is unlikely that an employee in the nuclear industry should be active in the Campaign for Nuclear Disarmament (CND).

Bringing the employer into disrepute

An employee submitted a fraudulent application for professional recognition. The offence was discovered when the professional body contacted the employer for confirmation of the employee's qualifications and experience.

The employee had represented himself as a senior engineer when, in fact, he was only an ordinary engineer. Furthermore he had described his experience as if he was actually a senior engineer.

The manager was extremely angry about the deception but uncertain what to do as he made the discovery by chance, and it is not directly concerned with the employee's role.

Once again, this case shows the importance of thinking critically about other people's definitions of reality. The manager did not come about the information by chance. The application was referred because it aroused suspicion. Besides, even if discovery had been accidental, what difference does it make? The police often discover criminals by chance but that hardly deters them from prosecuting. Furthermore, the incident must be related to the employee's role within the organisation. Otherwise, why would the manager be so concerned about it?

The real problem here is that the manager is so angry he is unable to find the words to express his concern. His concern is that the attempted deception reflects adversely upon the organisation which employs numerous engineers, many of whom apply for professional recognition.

Links between the employer and the professional body are close, reflecting their mutual interdependence. Not only has the employer been embarrassed by this incident, but, as a consequence, future applications for recognition will now probably be regarded suspiciously.

Even where faced with apparently incontrovertible evidence such as this, an investigation should always be conducted. There is always the possibility for instance that the forms may have become mixed up or some other error has occurred. Even if the evidence is accurate, there may be factors in mitigation.

In this instance the enquiry established that the employee had indeed submitted a fraudulent application. That is, he had been under no misapprehension concerning his role, nor had he misread the form, nor had he made any mistake in completing it. The mystery is why he committed the offence at all as his qualifications and experience as an ordinary engineer entitled him to professional recognition as they stood. This fact mitigated the offence as it was felt that although he had behaved dishonestly, it was not for gain. The engineer therefore received a written warning.

Media activity is another means of bringing an employer into disrepute. Media activity can be defined as any form of publication including writing to newspapers, writing stories, music and songs, or giving press interviews. The following factors are relevant in deciding if sanctions are appropriate:

- Whether publication is in the capacity as a private citizen, or as an employee.

- Whether the employee's role within the organisation can be readily inferred from the publication.

- Whether, and to what extent, the employer is criticised or otherwise harmed.

- The extent to which the employee has abused his position or divulged confidential information.

- Whether, and to what extent, the actual publication reflects the employee's understanding of what would appear.

It would be unfair to dismiss someone for media activity undertaken purely as a private citizen on a topic unrelated to their work or employing organisation. The exception might be if publication contravened some rule, though a tribunal would have to be satisfied that the regulation was necessary, specific and properly communicated.

Criticism of an employer by an employee in the media, whether express or implied, is a potential disciplinary matter depending upon whether the employee has abused his position and the employer, the extent of the damage and whether the employer's trust is destroyed.

Again, it is essential to investigate before acting because the employee may have been:

- put under pressure by the press;
- unaware that he would be quoted;
- quoted out of context;
- mis-represented.

Many organisations forbid employees from speaking to the press. It should always be remembered however that the tactics of some reporters and editors are sometimes dubious. It is by no means unknown for reporters to force their way into buildings and even concoct interviews. Innocuous information released in good faith may be totally distorted. Likewise, a mild letter written as a private citizen may be magnified into a headline sensation.

Other instances of harming the employer

Any outside activities which impact upon the employer's business are a potential concern. For instance:

A male designer became infatuated with a female secretary. Besides pestering her at work, he sent her expensive presents (all of which were returned), and then began telephoning her late at night and 'turning up' in the pubs and night clubs she frequented. On one occasion he followed her home and blocked her path with his motorcycle.

The atmosphere in the workplace has become extremely tense as essential communications and staff socialisation are disrupted.

The designer's manager however feels powerless as most of the incidents have occurred outside work.

The timing of the incidents is irrelevant as the resultant distress and tension are damaging organisational efficacy. Furthermore, the designer's conduct is tantamount to detrimental treatment within the meaning of the Sex Discrimination Act (see page 152). The employer is therefore obliged to intervene and even dismiss the designer if he persists.

Criminal activity unconnected with work

This too relates to conduct outside the workplace. However, it is such a big topic that it requires its own section. The term criminal activity here refers to instances where an employee has been either:

- convicted of an offence; or
- charged with an offence; or
- is suspected of criminal involvement.

Criminal involvement outside work is a legitimate concern if:

- it reflects adversely upon the employer; or
- it destroys his trust in the employee.

Employee convicted of an offence

The manager of an estate agency was fairly dismissed following a conviction for indecency with another man in a public toilet. Such were the effects of publicity in a small community, the organisation decided it would be harmful for business for the manager to continue working in the shop.

Cases such as this where there is a direct impact upon the employer are relatively easy to deal with. A dilemma occurs where the employee commits an offence which diminishes confidence, yet dismissal seems to be an over-reaction. For example:

> A social worker was convicted of possessing cannabis and fined £75. He said the drug was for his personal use only to relieve stress. The problem was that his job involved working with young people.

Clearly it is undesirable for a social worker employed with vulnerable clients to be convicted of a drugs offence. The problem for the employer is to balance a minor offence involving a soft drug against the possibility that for all he knows, the employee's private life may be inconsistent with his duties.

The first step is to interview the employee and any witnesses. Mere reliance upon a newspaper report is dangerous in that the report may be inaccurate, and equally important, background is usually omitted. This can be significant:

> The employee said that the cannabis was discovered in his car. He had been stopped and breathalised by police who had followed him from a night-club. The employee admitted that he was a regular patron there and that the club was a notorious haunt of prostitutes and drug dealers.

The employer must now ask himself whether, in the light of all the information, he can continue to trust the employee to work with young people? At the very least the employee must be warned about his behaviour. Dismissal may even be justified depending upon his record and length of service.

Employee charged with an offence

The principle of trust and confidence applies where an employee has only been charged with an offence:

> A parks' labourer was charged with sexually abusing his grandchild. His employers were concerned because of the potential danger of continuing to employ him in an environment where children play unsupervised. They wondered whether to suspend the employee pending his trial in six weeks' time.

The moral of this case is, never be panicked by other people into making a hasty decision or recommendation. The questions which should first be asked here are:

- Is the employee ever required to work unsupervised?
- What is the risk of a child being endangered?
- Could the employee be transferred?
- What would suspension achieve?
- What will happen if the employee receives a non-custodial sentence?
- What will happen if the employee is not convicted?
- How does the employee feel about what has happened?

The sole reason for suggesting suspension was the assumption that a lengthy custodial sentence would be imposed and so frustrate the contract thus relieving the employer of the problem. No one had actually considered the possibility of a probation order or what they would then do in the event. Furthermore, no one had talked to the employee. An interview subsequently revealed the following:

> The employee was shocked and horrified by what had happened. The incident had occurred over the weekend when the child came to stay with him. It was a single act quite out of character.
>
> He requested a transfer even though the only suitable vacancy entailed less pay. This, to him, was preferable to facing his workmates.

The dilemma for management was that should an incident have occurred at work newspaper headlines would doubtless read 'Council Shields Sex Maniac', and the like. Dismissal for SOSR might therefore have been admissible had it not been possible to transfer the employee to a post where he was not at risk. If dismissal had been contemplated (assuming the employee admitted the offence) no purpose would be served in waiting until his trial was concluded. The point is the employee was very nearly suspended and might have been sacked because no one had bothered to investigate. By so doing, a mutually acceptable solution was identified which obviated the need for any further action.

Refusal to work with an employee

A further concern in the preceding case was the possibility of an adverse reaction from other employees. Colleagues' refusal to work with an employee is an admissible reason for dismissal for SOSR though improper pressure from management is not. Moreover the refusal must be intractable, ie management must make reasonable efforts to integrate the employee and to persuade his colleagues to reconsider.

There is a difference between passive refusal to work with someone and violent protest. For example, throwing stones and clods of grass at a colleague is a disciplinary offence. The best way of handling such volatile situations before rushing into sanctions and the possibility of provoking industrial action, is to insist it stops immediately. Indeed, some managers would say that showing personal disapproval is more effective than taking disciplinary action.

Suspected criminal activity

It was emphasised in Chapter Two that employers should always investigate allegations of dishonesty regardless of whether police charges are to be brought. This applies to any criminal activity.

A Mr Strange was recently appointed as a training officer with special responsibility for counselling young people.

Shortly after his appointment, a female personnel officer reported that some months previously, Mr Strange had asked her if she was interested in appearing in blue movies. It was further reported that on his first day, Mr Strange had alarmed a female clerk by producing a snake from his pocket and placing it on her desk.

Mr Strange was interviewed about these incidents and stated that they were both intended as jokes.

Enquiries then revealed the existence of a police file on Mr Strange. The police refused to divulge the contents but intimated that Mr Strange had a long association with pornography. The council housing department indicated that there had been violent disturbance at Mr Strange's house because of his beating his wife.

Mr Strange was then suspended pending further investigation. Next, his wife appeared holding her baby, pleading on his behalf. She insisted that the rumours were nonsense. There was no sign of physical violence upon her. Mr Strange denied everything. No further information could be obtained.

Although Mr Strange's short service would have precluded recourse to a tribunal, he was a member of a powerful trade union who would have objected to capricious dismissal. Certainly the evidence was not completely satisfactory in that it was fragmentary and partly based on hearsay. Conversely however, the incident of the snake and the invitation to participate in pornography are disturbing. The former has sexual connotations while the police interest in Mr Strange suggests that his reference to blue movies was not entirely a joke. Moreover, the hearsay emanates from a reliable source. Taken together, the evidence suggests it would be unwise to retain Mr Strange in a position of trust. His trade union concurred with this conclusion and advised him to resign.

Summary and checklist

- In a disciplinary context, dismissal may be for conduct, performance or 'Some Other Substantial Reason' (SOSR).

- SOSR may be defined as anything sufficiently serious in the employer's eyes to warrant dismissal.

- An employee who is sent to prison does not automatically lose his job though he may be dismissed for SOSR or the contract may be frustrated.

- Failure to investigate allegations of sexual harassment may result in findings of constructive dismissal and sex discrimination.

- An employee must not:
  — compete with his employer;
  — make secret profits from his employment;
  — divulge confidential information or trade secrets.

- Violation of any obligation of fidelity may justify dismissal regardless of the damage caused if trust is destroyed.

- An employee is expected to devote all of his working hours to his employer's business.

- A second employment is permissible provided it does not:
  — significantly harm the employer;
  — affect the employee's ability to devote full attention and effort to his job;
  — contravene any express rule forbidding it.

- An employee's conduct outside work is his own business provided it does not:
  — conflict with his employment;
  — reflect adversely upon his employer;
  — harm the employer in any other way.

- All allegations of criminal activity should be investigated regardless of whether the police intend to prosecute.

- A criminal conviction unconnected with work may justify dismissal for SOSR if the employer's trust is destroyed.

- Dismissal for SOSR may be admissible even for suspected criminal activity if the employer's trust is destroyed.

Part Two
Preparing for a Disciplinary Hearing

Chapter Eight
Suspension in Practice

Introduction

The legal aspects of suspension were covered in the previous chapter. Essentially the law gives employers wide discretion to decide whether or not to suspend. The purpose of this chapter is to examine the advantages and disadvantages of suspension and to describe how to go about suspending an employee. As a general guide, suspension is essential where gross misconduct is involved but unwise for anything less.

When to suspend

Suspend an employee if:

- It is desirable that the employee should not continue to work until the case is decided.

- A cooling-off period is warranted.

- It is necessary to remove the employee from the workplace to facilitate an investigation.

Suspension is essential where gross misconduct is suspected because allowing an employee to continue working in these circumstances implies that dismissal is unnecessary. Suspension can be used to allow tempers to cool. Dismissal may be unfair if enacted hastily and a period of reflection might have resulted in a different decision. This applies with particular force to disobedience; the employee should always be given an opportunity to think matters through and retract. The following checklist may be useful in deciding whether suspension would facilitate an investigation.

Is suspension necessary to facilitate investigation? — Checklist

Is there reason to believe, if the employee continues to work normally that:

- Other employees may be persuaded or coerced into making false statements?

- Other employees may feel constrained from cooperating fully with enquiries?

- Further thefts or misdemeanours may be committed?

- Evidence may be destroyed or tampered with?

A positive answer to any of these questions is sufficient to justify suspension. Suspension significantly reduces the risk of employees closing ranks or being intimidated into silence. Likewise, suspension may release inhibitions, especially where the enquiry concerns the conduct of a manager or supervisor. Experience suggests that subordinates can be deeply reluctant to report superiors' misdeeds. For example, a supervisor had falsified his flexi-time records, leave bookings and car claims for years, yet was never reported because his staff were afraid of him. His misconduct only came to light when, during a job evaluation exercise, a personnel officer asked a junior employee how he got on with his supervisor. The office junior shuffled his feet and looked down. This suggested something amiss to the personnel officer. Gentle probing of other employees elicited similarly disturbing responses but no one would give any specific information. It was only after the supervisor was suspended that staff could bring themselves to report his conduct.

Where an employee is suspected of serious misconduct, he may perceive dismissal as inevitable and therefore that he has nothing to lose by perpetuating his offence for as long as possible. Unless it is practicable to transfer the employee to a position where he can do no harm, there may be no alternative but to suspend.

The following factors should be weighed up when assessing the risk of an employee destroying or tampering with evidence:

- What evidence is critical?

- Who supervises it?

- Do duplicates or secondary sources exist?

- Does the employee need access to it?

- What alternative arrangements can be made?

- Who else requires access to it?
- Can copies be made?
- What would be the consequences of tampering or destruction?

If an employee cannot work without access to evidence and if this cannot be secured in some way, or alternative arrangements made, suspension may be the only option.

Suspension as a device

Suspension can be used to regain the initiative in a conflict.

> A teacher took exception to a remark made by a colleague in the staff room which he felt was a slur upon his professionalism. He left the school there and then demanding that the headteacher deal with his grievance. The headteacher refused to act until the teacher returned. The teacher then asked the headteacher to visit him at home. The headteacher replied that any discussion must take place within the school. The teacher refused to return to the school.

The impasse was resolved by suspending the teacher pending a disciplinary hearing where he was dismissed for refusing to report for duty. Interestingly, had the teacher returned, the headteacher would have been obliged to investigate otherwise a claim for constructive dismissal might have been upheld if the remarks were truly detrimental. The headteacher was, however, quite correct in insisting that the teacher return to duty first. The proper thing would then have been to suspend the other teacher pending a hearing if the case was sufficiently serious.

When not to suspend

The disadvantages of suspension are:

- expense;
- the likelihood of an employee reporting sick;
- accusations of over-reacting; and
- problems in reinstating an employee.

Unless his contract says otherwise, an employee is entitled to full pay while suspended. Suspension therefore creates a non-productive burden upon overheads. Suspended employees are prone to develop protracted illnesses making it difficult to conclude proceedings to say nothing of the expense and other problems caused by absence. Particular caution is advised where serious criminal charges are likely, as in the case below.

A press report said that a college lecturer had been arrested by the police in connection with offences of indecency with young girls. The principal immediately wrote to the lecturer suspending him from duty pending an investigation. Bail restrictions were then imposed confining the lecturer to home.

Had the lecturer been interviewed, the possibility of confinement might have been foreseen. In seeking to avoid unpleasantness by suspending him by letter however, the college became liable to pay him until the case came to court nine months later.

It is important to maintain a sense of perspective in deciding whether or not to suspend. Although I know of no case law on the subject, it is conceivable that an unwarranted suspension could be tantamount to constructive dismissal if the employee's trust in his employer is destroyed. Furthermore, unnecessary suspension may upset industrial relations by being perceived as provocative and pre-emptive.

Where allegations prove unfounded or where proceedings result in a warning, suspension can make it difficult for an employee to return to work especially at professional and managerial levels, as this case shows.

A group of professional staff undertook a team-building course with an external consultant, as a result of which the consultant became aware of the staff's ill-feeling towards their manager. A report was submitted to the director indicating a serious breakdown in relationships. This included a covering letter stating '... perhaps there are still a few live cinders amongst the ashes'. The director was so alarmed that he suspended the manager forthwith.

The director's fast reaction was a mistake. Although the initial impact of the report was disturbing given comments such as '... staff appear to have lost confidence', and references to 'the deadness of morale', it actually contained little hard evidence. The director should have put it to one side for a day or so and then re-read it critically. He should then have compiled a list of questions such as what specific concerns had been identified and, what evidence was there to support these? For example, had the consultant conducted any form of systematic investigation or was he merely conveying his own impressions based on anecdote? On what basis did he conclude that relationships were about to break down?

The director should then have put these questions to the consultant face to face. Had he done so, he would have realised that the consultant hated the manager and therefore treated his report with even greater circumspection. Furthermore, it would have been clear that although some staff were unhappy, there was no evidence of an irretrievable collapse. The director could then have seen the manager about his performance. Instead, suspension was followed by a full-scale investigation which took four months to complete. This found that the manager had been uncontactable on two days (in two years) when supposedly working at home, and that he had attended a surprising number of funerals in this period. He had behaved aggressively on occasions towards clerical staff and had failed to communicate as effectively as he might. While these issues were a legitimate concern, they fell far short of grounds for dismissal. However, because of the time taken to complete the investigation and the stigma attached to the suspension, it seemed unrealistic and unfair to the manager to reinstate him. The result was a costly 'golden handshake'.

How to suspend an employee

Here is an example of how *not* to go about it:

> An employee was called to company headquarters to see a very senior manager. When he arrived, he was shown into an office where the manager and six assistants (all strangers) were waiting. Without even being asked to sit, he was told he was suspended. No further information was offered.

If you need to suspend someone, do so face to face with as few people present as possible. Unless procedures provide for it, no entitlement to representation exists. Equally, there is nothing to preclude it. The main thing is to be consistent, otherwise arguments may ensue over whether proper procedure was observed.

The interview may be brief, but should always convey the following information.

Suspending an employee — checklist
Tell the employee:

1. That you need to suspend him.
2. The reason for the suspension.
3. What will happen next, eg an investigation or a formal hearing.
4. The likely timescales.
5. That he will receive full pay while suspended (unless other contractual arrangements apply, in which case, explain these).
6. That he must not return to work until required to do so.
7. That he must be available if required.
8. That suspension is not a punishment nor does it imply that you have made your mind up in any way.

The interview is potentially stressful for all parties and therefore it is advisable to use this checklist to prepare for, and to guide you through, the interview and ensure that all points are covered.

Confirming suspension

Written confirmation is not obligatory but it is good practice and can prevent misunderstandings later. Again, be consistent. If issued, the letter or memo should incorporate all the numbered points contained in the checklist as follows:

Dear

①→ This is to confirm my interview with you today (in the presence of ——— if witnesses were present) suspending you from duty until further notice (state date if known).

②→ The reason for your suspension is to enable an investigation to take place into allegations of ———

③→ The allegations are of a potentially serious disciplinary nature and may result in your being required to attend a disciplinary hearing. If so, you will be notified in accordance with the company's disciplinary procedure.

④→ The investigation is likely to take a fortnight to complete and you may be required to attend a management interview in connection with the enquiry.

⑤→ You will receive full pay while suspended,

⑥→ but must not report for work unless instructed to do so.

⑦→ You must however be available to attend work at any time during normal working hours.

→ Suspension is not a punishment nor does it mean that you are regarded as guilty of the accusations. You will have every opportunity to state your case later should it be necessary.

Yours sincerely

If witnesses were present, the document should reflect this. At the end of the interview, tactfully escort the employee from the premises. Tact means not saying 'I must now escort you from the premises' when 'Come on, I'll see you out' will do just as well. Never allow an employee to return to his desk or give him any other opportunity to remove or interfere with evidence. Ask if there is anything he needs and fetch it for him.

You can instruct the employee to attend work at any time while suspended. He cannot therefore go on holiday or make himself otherwise unavailable without permission.

Summary and checklist

● Suspension is essential where gross misconduct is involved.

● Where less serious offences are involved, suspension should be used sparingly.

● Reasons for suspension are:
  — where it is undesirable for an employee to report for work until the case is concluded;
  — to allow tempers to cool;
  — to facilitate an investigation.

● Suspension can be used to regain the initiative in a conflict.

● The disadvantages of suspension are:
  — expense;
  — the likelihood of an employee reporting sick;
  — accusations of over-reacting;
  — potential problems of reinstatement.

● Beware of being over-hasty in suspending someone where serious criminal charges are likely.

● Suspension should be carried out in a face to face interview.

● Trade union representation is not obligatory unless specified in procedure; be consistent.

● The reason for, and terms of, the suspension should be explained to the employee.

- It is advisable to confirm suspension in writing: again, be consistent.

- Escort the employee from the premises.

- While suspended, the employee must make himself available as required.

Chapter Nine
The Role of a Management
Investigation

Introduction: why investigate?

A proper investigation is the key to applying disciplinary procedures successfully. This is because dismissal will only be upheld if an industrial tribunal is satisfied that reasonable grounds existed for a belief in an employee's guilt; meaning that decisions must reflect a fair and thorough investigation. Furthermore, precipitous action (whether legally valid or otherwise) can cause industrial relations problems.

Despite its fundamental importance, a surprising number of managers fail to devote adequate time to conducting an investigation, or regard the disciplinary hearing as the appropriate place to begin enquiries. Consequently, cases are lost needlessly and managers sometimes become discouraged from using proper procedures either resorting to underhand tactics or abdicating their responsibility for discipline, neither of which is conducive to maintaining morale and commitment.

It is appreciated that many managers and personnel officers can ill afford the time to investigate. There are no shortcuts however. Besides, a proper investigation often saves time in the long run as it results in better decisions, thereby reducing the likelihood of internal appeals, tribunal appearances and even industrial action. Furthermore, as this chapter will show, the role of an investigation is wider than providing a basis for a disciplinary hearing.

The role of an investigation

The functions of a management investigation are:

- To ascertain whether reasonable grounds exist for a belief in an employee's guilt.

- To protect employees from malice.

- To examine the effectiveness of organisational systems and procedures.

Each of these is now examined in detail.

Establishing a basis for belief in an employee's misconduct

A major role of a tribunal is to decide whether a reasonable investigation has taken place. Although no exact definition of the term *reasonable* exists, it can be said that an enquiry must be sufficiently thorough to enable an impartial outsider to conclude with confidence that the employee is guilty. The following two cases show how even simple disciplinary cases can be lost for want of an investigation.

Rogers was a member of the local communist party and well known for his extremist views and disruptive behaviour at work. He already had two warnings on file for unauthorised absence and excessive sickness. One Friday Rogers was missing at 3.30 pm though his shift was not due to finish until 4.00 pm. The following Monday, a disciplinary hearing was held. Rogers insisted that he had been at the back of the foreman's cabin sharpening his tools. Although no one believed him, the explanation was plausible and therefore the case was dismissed. Rogers then filed a grievance for victimisation.

Alas, management did not even ask to inspect Rogers' tools. This alone might have discredited his story. Besides, as soon as Rogers' absence was noted, someone should have positively established that he was not on site, preferably with a witness. An investigatory interview should then have taken place on the Monday. Had this been done, management's evidence might have read:

At 3.30 pm I noticed Mr Rogers was missing. I systematically searched the whole site working from the gate inward. I did not see Mr Rogers anywhere. I could not have missed him as he would have had to pass me on his way out. Mr Smith accompanied me.

I asked Mr Rogers to account for his absence at a management interview on Monday morning. He said he had been at the back of the cabin sharpening his tools. I replied that Mr Jones the foreman and I had searched the area behind the shed and he was not there. I then asked Mr Rogers to produce his tools ...

The next case shows the danger of jumping to conclusions:

An employee was seen drinking in a pub by his manager despite a strict rule forbidding consumption of alcohol during working hours.

At the disciplinary hearing the employee admitted being in the pub but said that his mother had died recently, and, that he had suddenly become tearful. He went to the pub to buy a brandy to help him compose himself.

Despite their better judgement, management had to accept the employee's explanation. The outcome might have been different had he been challenged holding a pint of beer in his hand.

The role of an investigation in protecting innocent employees

Part of the function of an investigation is to set allegations in perspective and so protect employees from exaggeration or malice, as will become apparent through the following case.

A manager received an angry telephone call from two customers, a lady in her eighties and her 60-year-old daughter. They alleged that an apprentice decorator (a girl) had left their flat in a disgraceful mess. They were furious and had arranged for the local newspaper to come and photograph the 'pigsty' 'she' (the apprentice) had left.

Correctly, the manager decided to see for himself before interviewing the apprentice. He found that although she had omitted to use dust sheets and that there were a few splashes of emulsion (which the girl had said she would clean next day), the standard of work was acceptable. As the manager talked to the two old ladies, the real reason for their upset emerged. First they were nonplussed to see a woman painter, and one so young. Second, they were distressed when she declined their offers of tea and scones saying that she had better get on with the job. With nothing else to occupy them, the two women had allowed their disappointment to ferment.

The manager saw the apprentice next day, reminded her about the dust sheets and then explained, without any implication or criticism, that it would be better if someone else finished off the job. To the old ladies he said 'Don't worry, I'll send someone round in the morning.'

> A female employee alleged that the company doctor had required her to remove her bra and lie down on the examination couch and then had 'ogled' her.

Little imagination is required to appreciate the rumours which circulated in the organisation as news of this complaint emerged. The doctor had been chaperoned. He had not been chaperoned. He had been chaperoned but the chaperon was lying to protect him. The brassiere had been removed. It had not been removed. Removal was clinically necessary; it was not clinically necessary.

Here failure to investigate could result in a claim for constructive dismissal. The doctor could argue that the employer allowed his credibility and integrity to be destroyed and thereby violated the relationship of trust and confidence.

In fact, the investigation confirmed that the doctor had been properly chaperoned, that the examination was clinically necessary, and that it had been conducted with the employee standing. The bra was not removed, only loosened. Furthermore, the employee had arrived 40 minutes late and admitted that the doctor's irritation had prompted the complaint.

Malicious allegations such as these constitute misconduct. The penalty depends upon their seriousness, whether the employee is motivated by gain and the vigour with which they are pursued. The accusations here were extremely serious, and would always cast doubt over the doctor's integrity even though unfounded. Moreover the employee's conduct was such as potentially to destroy the employer's trust in her. Dismissal would therefore have been a reasonable response. However, as the complaint was made in the heat of the moment and subsequently retracted with an unreserved apology, a final warning resulted.

The role of an investigation in evaluating organisational systems and procedures

The discovery of misconduct frequently signals weaknesses in organisational systems and procedures. Part of the function of an investigation is to analyse these and to recommend changes.

> A consignment of cooked beef was left standing uncovered in a kitchen for several hours on a hot day. It was then served and caused an outbreak of food poisoning.

Although the person who left the food out was directly responsible for the outbreak, the investigation concluded that the real cause was inadequate staffing. Catering staff worked under pressure and therefore took shortcuts whenever they could, eventually with disastrous consequences.

A care assistant was dismissed after posing as a home help and stealing approximately £30,000 from elderly clients.

Preventing a recurrence of this offence is more important than dealing with the individual. The investigation revealed a complete lack of basic security precautions. The offender was able to obtain names and addresses from the files without question. No identity cards were issued. It was a reflection upon supervision that it took two years to identify the thief.

When should an investigation take place?

Investigations must always be held promptly before recollections fade. The investigation should be concluded before the disciplinary hearing because:

- it reduces the possibility of surprise defences;

- enquiries can be conducted much more easily;

- the disciplinary process is more likely to operate smoothly and fairly;

- the employee is spared distress if the allegations are unfounded; and

- management time can be saved.

The significance of these points is best illustrated by example.

A woman complained that a workman had been 'over familiar' with her. She was interviewed and gave an account of what took place. At the disciplinary hearing the employee pointed out that an apprentice had been working with him that day. The apprentice confirmed this. The complainant's account however contained no reference to an apprentice.

Not only was this a surprise defence but proceedings were disrupted and time wasted through calling an adjournment to enable the apprentice to appear. The trade unions were scathing about the inadequacy of the investigation and threatened industrial action if their member was subjected to any further distress by reopening enquiries.

Summary and checklist

- A proper investigation is the key to fairness.

- Even the simplest of cases requires proper investigation.

- The main purpose of an investigation is to provide evidence for a belief in an employee's guilt.

- Investigations also serve to:
  - protect employees from malice; and
  - improve effectiveness.

- The investigation should be concluded before a disciplinary hearing is convened.

Chapter Ten
Carrying Out an Investigation

Introduction

The previous chapter emphasised the need for a proper investigation in order to substantiate a belief in an employee's guilt. If your conclusions are to persuade others, your approach must be:

- planned; and
- thorough.

This chapter examines what each of these points means in practice.

A strategy for conducting an investigation

A useful motto for investigators is 'Don't just do something, stand there'.* Before rushing out to interview witnesses or conduct observations you should first ask yourself:

- what is my concern; and
- what do I need to know?

Establishing a concern

All investigations begin with a concern over conduct or capability. The concern may emanate from personal experience or it may arise from a newspaper article, an anonymous letter, a written complaint or a report from another employee.

The concern must be defined clearly as it is the foundation of the investigation. This applies to even the simplest of cases.

---

* I am unaware of the origin of this saying. I first heard it from my former colleagues Tom Clinton and Bernard McEvoy.

A manager driving past a public house one lunch-time sighted an employee's vehicle in the car park. He drove on to a telephone box and contacted the site who confirmed that the employee was missing. The manager then went back to the pub but found the car was gone. He then drove to the employee's house and saw a car similar to that in the pub car park outside. He then knocked at the door and suspended the employee for being in a pub while on duty, a dismissable offence.

At the disciplinary hearing, the employee denied being in the pub. Since even if it was the employee's car the manager had seen, it did not necessarily mean that the owner was in the pub, the employee escaped with a warning for unauthorised absence.

In fact, the manager should have entered the pub as soon as he saw the car and challenged the employee. The manager said he did not do so because he was not absolutely certain it was the employee's car and because he did not have a witness with him. Yet what would have been lost had he been mistaken? A witness is not essential, for how could the employee subsequently deny he had been in the pub if his manager had actually challenged and suspended him there?

In his eagerness to prosecute, the manager had confused the subsidiary concern of unauthorised absence with the much more serious one of being on licensed premises. Consequently the succeeding steps of his investigation were flawed.

What do I need to know? — formulating a strategy for an investigation

Having clarified the concern, you must then consider what evidence is required to substantiate your *prima facie* belief in the employee's guilt. In other words, an effective investigation requires a plan. Here is an example of an enquiry embarked upon without thinking through the nature of the concern or how to pursue it.

A manager received an anonymous telephone call alleging that an employee who had been off work for three months with back strain was working in his own newsagent's shop.

Next day, the manager drove to the shop at 6.45 pm and observed the employee serving a customer. He revisited next morning at 7.45 am accompanied by a witness and saw the employee with a newspaper bag over his shoulder. When they entered the shop the employee was gone. The other person serving behind the counter said 'He's out'. The two managers went back to their car and kept watch on the shop for another hour. The employee did not reappear.

At a subsequent management interview the employee denied he had been in the shop that morning. He claimed he had been walking the dog. The employee was subsequently dismissed for 'Working while off sick'.

The employee's case at the industrial tribunal was:

- He was bored at home but fit enough to help out in the shop occasionally.

- He produced medical certificates indicating he was incapable of carrying out his regular duties as a joiner but that light work such as serving behind a counter would facilitate recovery.

- He produced evidence to show that the shop belonged to his wife from whom he was separated and living at another address. He was not, he said, gaining financially from the arrangement.

- Nothing in his contract forbade secondary employment for gain or otherwise.

There were, however, inconsistencies in the employee's story. For example, first he denied being in the shop on the morning he was seen by his manager. Later he suggested that the paper bag he was seen carrying over his shoulder was empty. (In fact, he was probably about to depart on a paper round to cover for an absentee delivery boy.) Despite these contradictions, the tribunal found there were insufficient grounds upon which to base a belief in misconduct.

Management would have been more successful had they first confirmed that there were *prima facie* grounds for concern by making one or

187

two unobtrusive observations and then paused to plan their approach and define their concern precisely. The latter may seem obvious but little credibility was gained at the tribunal for dismissing the employee for 'Working while off sick . . .' when what was really meant was abuse of the sick pay scheme, or breach of contract. Furthermore, mis-defining the concern resulted in an inadequate investigation because management thought it would be sufficient to show that the employee had worked while claiming sick pay.

The next question which should have been asked was what evidence is needed to convince a reasonable person that on the balance of probabilities, abuse is being committed? The best way to answer this question is to imagine you are the employee. What would you say if accused? The employee's case here was both plausible and predictable. Management should therefore have mounted an effective counter strategy by:

- Conducting sufficient observations over a reasonable period and at different times to show that the employee was serving in the shop all day, every day.

- Obtaining detailed advice from the company doctor. Back complaints are notoriously difficult to disprove. Management should have ascertained whether the employee's condition could easily be faked, and, whether someone genuinely injured could or should serve in a shop.

- Arranging a medical examination before confronting the employee. This would destroy any defence that his condition had recently improved. Indeed, he might have incriminated himself by telling the doctor that he could hardly stand!

With hindsight (the only exact science known to man), given the evidence available, it would have been better to pave the way to dismissal by issuing a warning. Alternatively a ploy might have been to assign the employee to light duties without making any reference to his retail activities. Dismissal would be more easily justified had he declared himself unfit for light work and then been observed serving behind the counter.

Planning an investigation

Having identified the concern and asked yourself 'What do I need to know?', develop your approach by setting down answers to the following.

Planning an investigation — checklist

- Do I need to familiarise myself with any background or technical information?

- What documents should I see?

- Who do I need to see?

- In what order?

- What questions do I need to ask?

- What answers do I expect?

The checklist should be seen as providing a rough map to facilitate a systematic approach, to ensure that no obvious step is missed and to measure progress. An enquiry is a dynamic process requiring frequent review and re-planning. The exercise should therefore be repeated as new leads emerge and the focus of attention changes.

A sound grasp of technical or other relevant specialist information is necessary if you are to make sense of your findings and communicate these to others. For example, you may need to study the operation of a warehouse or a production system or familiarise yourself with accounting conventions, computer software and the like.

Many enquiries require study of documentation ranging from examining an employee's file to analysing volumes of reports, invoices, correspondence and so on. Before beginning, ask yourself what should be available? The absence of one document may be more significant than the presence of the remaining hundred or more.

Failure to interview an obvious witness will almost certainly render a dismissal unfair. Compiling a preliminary list of people you need to see will reduce the likelihood of this happening. The list will probably grow as enquiries progress.

Think through and jot down the questions you need to ask. Initially there will probably be very few; even so, preparation maximises effectiveness. Take for example this extract from a letter:

> He came back on the Monday morning and pinned me to the wall and tried to kiss me.

Part of the function of an investigation is to enable a dispassionate outsider to understand exactly what happened. Here, among other questions, the investigator needs to ask:

- What time on Monday did 'he' arrive?

- How did he get in?

- What did he say when you answered the door?

This is not to suggest that the interview should be confined to asking pre-determined questions. The next chapter emphasises the importance of a free hand approach. At the same time however, you must ensure that essentials are covered.

It is advisable to note not only what you must do but why. This can be a useful source of reference in a complex investigation. Furthermore it provides protection against claims of harassment if you can recollect the reason for your actions.

Personal survival

Investigators are often distracted from their regular job for prolonged periods and subjected to abnormal stress and hostility. For your own survival, ensure arrangements are made to cover your regular work while you are engaged elsewhere. If necessary, set a time aside each day to visit the office to attend to urgent business. Ensure others know when you will be available. Pay particular attention to relaxation and receiving support from friends and family.

Summary and checklist

- An investigation must be planned and thorough.

- A useful motto for investigators is 'Don't just do something, stand there'.

- Begin by defining your concern, this is the foundation for everything else.

- Before embarking on enquiries, ask yourself 'what do I need to know?'

- A good way of planning an investigation is to imagine you are the suspect.

- The plan should set out in detail what needs to be done, in what order and why.

- The plan should be revised as new leads emerge.

- Pay attention to your own survival by making arrangements to cover your regular duties and for social support.

Chapter Eleven
Investigating Documentary Evidence

Introduction

It is a good idea to begin enquiries by inspecting documentary evidence. This is because this task can normally be accomplished discreetly, without arousing suspicion prematurely or causing upset should your concerns prove unfounded. Moreover, documents may yield clues to guide your enquiries or even provide direct evidence of misconduct. It may be necessary to examine additional documents later, but begin with whatever is immediately relevant.

A systematic approach to handling documents

When dealing with documents always:

- Label everything clearly.

- Retain source material or obtain a good photocopy.

- Compile a list of all material.

- File everything methodically.

A clear labelling system indicates meticulousness and therefore creates a good impression upon tribunals, lawyers, trade union officials and so forth. It will also save considerable time and confusion as what begins as a simple enquiry can burgeon into one involving several hundred sheets of paper.

Always retain either the original or a good copy of everything you examine whether or not you anticipate using it as evidence. Something initially inconsequential may become significant later. This is particularly important where criminal activity is suspected as the police may sequester documents. Prompt copying may enable you to proceed without waiting months (or even years) for their return. Incidentally, it can be revealing to photocopy documents before announcing the instigation of an enquiry. For example, a domestic bursar was suspected of over-ordering food and selling the surplus. The menu sheets were discreetly photocopied, witnessed and signed. An investigation was then launched and when the originals were re-inspected, they had been drastically amended.

Compile a list of documents as you go and check off those you have examined. This will enable you to tell at a glance what has been covered and save repeating work by mistake. Furthermore, should anything be removed you will know. In complex cases, cross-referencing in subject and numerical order will facilitate retrieval of information. All documentation should therefore be kept in a secure place.

What to look for when investigating documents

Be on the look out for any of the following:

- alterations;
- tears;
- use of pencil;
- unusual stains;
- unusual smells;
- inserts and Sellotapings;
- photocopies among originals;
- use of correction fluid;
- over-writing; and
- anything else unusual.

Alterations and tears are always suspicious. Ask yourself, why anyone would want to do that. Look further, is there a pattern, are alterations all by the same person for example, do tears occur regularly and if so, at what intervals? Use of pencil may be a convenient way of concealing amendments and erasures. Stains and smells may indicate that the document has been removed from the workplace, taken home perhaps. Again, ask yourself why was that necessary? Inserts, photocopies and Sellotape all suggest tampering and are particularly suspicious if they occur systematically. Use of correction fluid warrants investigation — does it conceal something, and if so, what? Hold papers up to the light.

Has anything been over-written? People have been known to fill fountain pens with correction fluid and to rewrite whole sets of records to conceal fraud.

Curiosity often pays dividends. Always do a little more than the bare minimum. For example, inspect not only the particular sheet of a receipt book or flexitime record you are concerned with, but look through the whole book. Examine backdated records perhaps. Do not allow preoccupation with detail to detract from making general observations. Is it a well-kept book, for example, up to date and so forth? Watch out for anything unusual or inconsistent. For example, a record book in mint condition is inconsistent with it having been completed on the shop floor. Most likely you are looking at a duplicate; if so, where was it copied and why? Similarly a neat and tidy sheet among crude working documents is suspicious.

Understanding documents in context

It is essential to understand the function of all documentation in order to appreciate its significance in the context of the investigation and, in particular, to draw inferences and identify clues. The following checklist can be used as a basis for enquiries.

Systems and procedures — checklist

- Who is responsible for completing the documentation?
- What does this involve?
- How long does it take?
- Why is it necessary?
- Where does this procedure fit within the system?
- Where are records kept?
- For how long are they kept?
- How are they disposed of?
- Who else has access to the documentation?
- Why?
- Who is responsible for supervising?
- What is the level of supervision?

It may also be fruitful to find out whether anyone else has interested themselves in the procedure. Imagine, for example, that you discover a clerk is responsible for issuing and maintaining purchase accounts under the direct supervision of a senior clerk and the office manager. Suppose you then learn that the chief accountant took the ledger home and lost it. Your knowledge makes you suspicious — what need was there to check a routine and well-supervised procedure? What other reason might exist for their removal?

Examining the contents of the document

Another function of the preceding analysis is to identify any weaknesses in security. It is often said that the surest way to catch a thief is to think like a thief. How would you conceal your crime? What flaws in the system might you exploit? Before perusing a document, therefore, ask yourself what do I expect to see? Knowing what you are looking for makes it easier to detect fraud or other irregularities especially if detailed and complex cross-checking is entailed. Then work through the document carefully and systematically checking any arithmetic and also any dates against a perpetual calendar.

Investigating anonymous letters

Anonymous communications should always be investigated. Careful and methodical examination can yield clues about the author's identity and help interpret the message. Proceed as outlined in the following checklist.

Examining anonymous letters — checklist

- Note the date, time and place of posting.
- Examine the condition of the envelope.
- Note to whom it is addressed.
- Examine the paper.
- Study the handwriting or typescript.
- Study the contents of the message.
- Examine the use of English and forms of expression.

Date, time and place of posting are unlikely to lead instantly to the author but may help identify him later. If the letter was hand-delivered then this narrows the possibilities. A communication addressed to a particular official or employee may mean that the author has some knowledge of the organisation.

Examine the condition of the envelope, are there any grease or other stains? If so, could they have come from anywhere within the organisation? Smell is important, note for example whether there is any suggestion of tobacco, oil, perfume or leather. Has the envelope been carried in the pocket of a workman's donkey jacket or in an executive's briefcase? Does any fragrance suggest a male or female author? Is the smell a familiar one?

An affluent person may use a common brand of stationery to conceal his identity. Someone less well off however will rarely purchase expensive stationery. Is the paper similar to anything used in the organisation? If the letter has been produced in typescript or on a computer printer does it match any office machines? Old typewriters for example often produce a distinctive script. Use of a laser printer narrows the field of suspects. If the letter is handwritten, note the type of pen. Biro is seldom distinctive but it is worth examining whether the colour, width and quality of script corresponds to anything that is standard issue within the organisation. If a fountain or roller-ball pen has been used, bear this in mind. Later on you may see someone with such a pen.

Any attempt to disguise handwriting suggests that the author is either known to people in the organisation or is likely to become known. The general style of handwriting and any peculiarities should be noted. While superficial disguise is achievable, careful examination of detail such as methods of dotting i's and crossing t's and letter formation may enable the author to be identified. Writing pressure is extremely difficult to change. Misuse of English may be a ploy by a literate person to pose as an illiterate. The reverse however is impossible. Spelling mistakes should be noted.

Having thus gained some idea as to the identity of the author, the contents of the message should then be studied. Even the most generalised of statements may yield clues to guide the investigation. For instance:

Dear

I wonder if you know how your organisation is run? Everyone thieving bastards at Green Tree Lane Depot.

From,

A Friend

The word 'everyone' suggests widespread corruption possibly involving supervisors as well as operatives. The term 'thieving' as distinct from 'nicking' or 'robbing' suggests organised theft especially when taken in conjunction with the word 'bastards' which follows. Obvious possibilities as to the identity of the author are an ex-employee, someone living near the depot or someone having contact with it but not actually working there.

A check on personnel records showed someone had left recently though the handwriting did not match. The ex-employee was however interviewed at home. Idly curious, the investigator glanced at a note on the kitchen calendar penned by the employee's wife. Although the handwriting in the letter had been disguised, the shape of the letters corresponded with those on the calendar.

Summary and checklist

- It is a good idea to begin an investigation by examining documentary evidence first.

- Always label and store documents systematically, even if there are only a few.

- When examining documents watch out for anything unusual or suggestive or alterations or tampering.

- Familiarise yourself with the systems and procedures pertaining to documentation. Look out for weaknesses in security.

- To catch a thief, think like a thief.

- When scrutinising records ask yourself 'what do I expect to find?'

- Anonymous communications should always be investigated. Careful study may help identify the author, and interpret the message.

Chapter Twelve
Interviewing a Witness

Introduction

Most investigations involve interviewing witnesses. Since disciplinary enquiries often take place in an emotive atmosphere, this is a task calling for particular skill. This chapter explains how to conduct an interview and how to cope with some of the problems which sometimes arise during investigations such as:

- What if an employee refuses to sign a statement?

- What if an employee admits to an offence and then denies it later?

- What if an employee refuses to say anything?

- What if a member of the public who is a key witness refuses to cooperate?

- What if children are involved?

- What if a witness goes sick?

Why interview witnesses?

An interview may be defined as a conversation with a purpose. In a disciplinary context the purpose is to obtain a full, written account of what took place, known as a statement.

All statements must be obtained in a personal interview. Shortcuts such as leaving a witness to write down what he knows are invariably counter-productive. The resultant information will be partial, unauthenticated and consequently, unreliable. Moreover, it reflects badly upon the investigator's competence and diligence, as the next case demonstrates.

A householder complained to a foreman that a workman had broken his clothes-pole by carelessly throwing blocks of rotten timber from a roof. The foreman asked the householder to write down what had happened. Two hours later a disciplinary hearing was held. The workman denied the allegation. He said that he had hit the pole accidentally with his ladders. The base was rotten and therefore the pole snapped. Despite his denial, the workman was summarily dismissed for wilful violation of health and safety regulations.

Predictably, the tribunal found that the speed with which dismissal was enacted precluded any possibility of a proper investigation. Someone should have interviewed the householder to discover the full picture instead of just relying upon a brief note. For example, where was he standing at the time and what exactly did he see?

Who should be interviewed?

A witness is defined as anyone potentially in possession of relevant information. It is essential to interview all witnesses as they may be able to shed light upon the credibility of other witnesses even though new information emerges.

Powers of an interviewer

Although no general duty to report misdeeds exists, an employee can be required to account for his stewardship. That is, to answer questions pertaining to his job including conduct outside the organisation if relevant. This implies cooperating with enquiries, attending management interviews and so on. An effective interviewer, however, depends less upon wielding power authority and more on utilising interpersonal skills to develop rapport and confidence with witnesses. We now examine how this can be achieved.

Interview techniques

Rarely does it help for interviewers to emulate the Spanish Inquisition. Essentially a management interview should be assertive without being aggressive, and, purposeful without being officious. Key steps to effectiveness are:

1. Show a personal interest in the respondent and concern for his feelings.
2. Use positive reinforcement to encourage the respondent to talk by saying things like 'That's good' and 'That's interesting'.
3. Be gentle, the hardest of questions can be asked in the softest of voices.
4. Never show disapproval — whatever the respondent tells you.
5. Avoid sarcasm; it is hurtful, unfair and seldom productive.
6. Use silence to force the respondent to speak and to allow him collect his thoughts.
7. Avoid physical contact or making personal remarks.
8. Maintain a relaxed body posture and eye contact.

Effective interviewing requires purposefulness combined with a relaxed and friendly manner. Always retain the initiative but do so subtly, for example by holding the interview on your territory, controlling seating arrangements, supplying coffee and so forth.

People tend to be attracted to, and prefer to cooperate with, those who display warmth and concern towards them. A soft approach can be extremely successful in overcoming resistance. Some of the most successful policemen use gentleness to the point where the person under arrest comes to believe that he is their best friend.

Try and help the respondent over difficult or potentially embarrassing admissions. Maintain a matter-of-fact demeanour and be supportive by saying for example 'You must be glad to have got that off your chest'. However shocked or angry you feel about what the respondent tells you, never appear to judge or communicate disapproval. In particular, guard against betraying censure in your eyes. It will be noticed by the respondent and discourage him.

Restrain yourself from talking when the respondent falls silent. Silence creates a vacuum and therefore the natural impulse is to fill it. Forcing the respondent to speak can lead to interesting results. For example:

Q. Did you shout at the patient?
A. No.

Silence

A. I mean I might have raised my voice a little . . .

Silence

A. I mean, we're all human aren't we . . .'

Silence

A. We all blow our top sometimes don't we . . .

To test the power of the technique of silence, read this dialogue aloud allowing a ten-second pause at the end of every juncture. It is almost possible to feel oneself filling the vacuum. After 30 seconds it becomes unendurable.

Silence also enables the respondent to collect his thoughts which may enable him to remember something important or introduce new information which would otherwise be suppressed by a constant stream of questions.

How to approach a management interview

An effective interview consists of the following four phases:

1. Establishing rapport and confidence.
2. Preliminary questions.
3. The interview proper.
4. Relaxing.

The process of establishing rapport begins when actually arranging the interview. The easiest way to obtain a statement is not to ask for one. The term 'statement' with its connotations of police enquiries and court proceedings is alarming and should therefore be avoided. Don't say:

> I wish to obtain a statement from you in connection with a serious disciplinary enquiry . . .

as you may frighten the respondent and make him defensive. Instead begin with:

> Hello, my name is ————. The chief executive has asked me to look into ————. I will be seeing all of the staff and I wondered if you could help me . . .

A low-key approach minimises tension. At the start of the interview concentrate on developing a relationship with the respondent by displaying interest in him and offering reassurance. Preliminary questions should be simple, factual and non-contentious; questions which the respondent can answer easily. These should include background information about the respondent's job, length of service and key responsibilities. From these, lead gradually into the substance of the enquiry beginning with simple questions of fact then, slowly, begin to probe.

Using open questions to develop a story

Note taking at this stage is counter-productive because it impedes the flow of information. Concentrate on getting the respondent to talk and, as you listen, keep asking yourself:

- what does he know; and
- how does he come to know it?

Open questions, (who, what, where, when and why?) are the best means of developing the story. For instance:

- *What* do you mean by that?
- *When* did that happen?
- *Where* were you at the time?
- *What* did he say?
- *How* do you know?
- *Why* did he do that?
- *Who* told you?
- *What* did they say?
- *How* did they know?
- *Why* were you there?
- *Did* anyone else see *what* happened?
- *Where* were they at the time?
- *What* did they say?
- *What* happened after that?

Making sense of the interview

Initially the information will be fragmented and the sequence disjointed. The interviewer's task is to order the story by memorising key points. This may sound daunting without the aid of notes but statements rarely contain more than five or six crucial points. Memorising these requires intense concentration but it can be done.

The story is complete when, despite probing, nothing new emerges. Now summarise the story and then reflect it back to the respondent, point by point. This enables you to check the details and shows the respondent that you have listened to him. Indeed, this may be the first time he has actually heard the account for himself! Now produce your pen and say something like 'Let me jot this down whilst it's still fresh in our minds'. What you are actually doing is writing out the statement.

Compiling a statement

A written statement is the only means of satisfying others that a proper investigation has taken place. The statement should be compiled in long hand, in the presence of the respondent. Statements must reflect the respondent's own words, otherwise they will appear contrived and may be challenged.

The statement should indicate:

- The date, time and place of the interview.

- Who is making the statement.

- Their job title.

- A brief summary of their responsibilities especially in relation to the subject of the investigation.

- A sequential account of events with dates, times, and places sufficiently detailed to enable an outsider to understand what happened.

The statement should begin as follows:

> My name is Peter Smith and I have been employed as a technician in the computer department since 1989. One of my main responsibilities is to maintain a file of computer passwords for security purposes.

This biographical information enables the reader to identify who is giving the statement, what their job is and how long they have been employed. This information also indicates the level at which the respondent is employed and the extent of his experience. The description of key responsibilities alerts the reader to the nature of the enquiry. Furthermore, it is evidence that the respondent understands his role. This may be significant if the enquiry reveals that he has been negligent.

Compiling the main body of the statement

A description of events then follows in chronological order:

> On Monday 22 June 1989 at 2.00 pm I was carrying out a routine security check and noticed that someone from the purchasing department had been using a password which belonged to the personnel department. I immediately told my supervisor, Mr Lillywhite, but he said it was OK.

> At the time I thought this was a funny thing to say but I didn't say anything as I had only been in the department for three weeks. Then, on Monday 8 July during another routine security check I noticed that the same thing had happened again. This time, when I told Mr Lillywhite, he got upset . . .

Note how each major point (or phase of the story) is contained in a separate paragraph with dates, times and places incorporated. It is unlikely that the story will have been told in such an orderly fashion. Most probably, it began by the respondent making some vague reference to his supervisor's idiosyncratic behaviour which was then probed by the interviewer.

Signing the statement

Once the statement is complete, it should be read aloud to the respondent. Again, a relaxed approach helps keep the respondent at ease. You might for example say 'Just see if this makes sense ... interrupt me if I've got anything wrong'. At the end of each paragraph make eye contact with the respondent and seek confirmation by saying 'OK?' or 'Have I got that right?'.

The respondent should then sign the statement and initial any amendments. Rarely will he object because the process of developing and reflecting back the story transfers psychological ownership from the respondent to the interviewer. If the respondent does object ask him why. If you are unable to persuade him to sign, note the reason for the refusal on the statement and sign it yourself.

Closing the interview

Wherever possible, close the interview on a positive note by thanking the respondent for his help and by checking whether he feels he has had a fair and full interview. Round off with a few social pleasantries. If asked what the outcome will be, just say that you do not know.

The statement should then be typed. The respondent need not sign the copies but do ensure that the original is kept secure.

It is always possible that a witness will subsequently retract all or part of a statement or accuse you of behaving improperly. The presence of a management witness is therefore useful. However, if it can be shown that the interview was carried out in accordance with the preceding recommendations, it is unlikely that a hearing or tribunal will attach much credence to a retraction or complaint.

No rights to trade union representation at management interviews exist unless provided for by disciplinary procedures. The main thing is to be consistent; if you allow representation once, allow it always, unless it is clearly on the basis of an *ad hoc* agreement.

Re-interviewing a witness

Usually one interview will suffice provided it is sufficiently thorough.

However, it is essential to pursue any new leads if you are to convince others that a proper investigation has taken place. The process described above should be repeated for every interview and separate statements compiled.

Interviewing a hostile witness

A hostile witness is defined as someone not expected to cooperate with enquiries. In the context of disciplinary proceedings, the employee accused of misconduct should be regarded as a hostile witness.

A different approach is required to interview a hostile witness, that is:

- Questions are pre-prepared.

- The interview consists of a question and answer session.

- Each answer is recorded before proceeding to the next question.

- Two interviewers are required.

- The interviewers sign the statement, not the employee.

Since there is little prospect of the respondent talking openly and freely, specific questions are necessary. It is, therefore, best to see hostile witnesses last, as the interview is usually based upon information obtained earlier. Since there is little chance of being able to develop a story, answers are recorded there and then. The second interviewer acts as witness and scribe. The interviewers sign because it is their statement, not the employee's.

Preparing to interview a hostile witness

Compile a question sheet leaving ample room to record responses and for supplementary questions to be added. You may already know most, if not all, of the answers: the art is to use your information to demonstrate the employee's guilt. A specimen statement is shown below:

My name is Peter Smith. I am company personnel officer and have served in that capacity since 1989. One of my responsibilities is maintenance of security.

On 7 June I was called to the managing director's office and asked to conduct an enquiry into allegations concerning theft of computer equipment.

In pursuance of this enquiry I interviewed Mr Lillywhite, the computer manager. I asked Mr Lillywhite to describe events immediately prior to the disappearance of a consignment of computer hardware on 26 June 1989.

1. Q. Were you on duty that night?
   A. Don't know.
2. Q. I have the time-book here which shows you clocked on at eight o'clock. Do you care to comment on that?
   A. No comment.
3. Q. Whose responsibiity is it to sign delivery notes?
   A. No comment.
4. Q. I have a copy of your job description here which says it's your responsibility. What have you to say?
   A. [Shrug of shoulders] Don't care.
5. Q. What is the purpose of a delivery note?
   A. Not sure.
6. Q. Is it to verify goods have been received?
   A. Something like that.
7. Q. Do you recognise this delivery note? [Note shown]
   A. No.
8. Q. What does it refer to?
   A. Computers, stupid, can't you read?
9. Q. Is this your signature?
   A. Don't know.
10. Q. Is it or isn't it?
    A. Suppose so.

Conducting the interview

The preamble to the statement can be written out in advance. Note how the investigator has done his homework and is using the information to confront the employee. The time-book has been examined, delivery notes checked and so forth.

Refusals or reluctance to explain should be noted and the question repeated. This shows that the employee has had a fair chance to respond. If he still refuses to answer, note the fact and move onto the next question. It is immaterial if the respondent is negative or evasive — what impression does Mr Lillywhite create? Similarly, abuse and provocation will soon cease when the respondent sees it being written down!

At the end of the interview, read the statement slowly to the respondent. Ask him to indicate any inaccuracies. Then, in the presence of the respondent, you and your colleague should sign the statement. It is not necessary for the respondent to sign as the statement is your account of the interview, not his.

Confessions

If a hostile witness volunteers a statement, it should be recorded word for word. Incidentally, it is dangerous to rely upon confessions alone. All witnesses should be interviewed and other evidence investigated.

Obtaining a statement from a member of the public

A member of the public is under no obligation to give a statement. An interview should always be sought, however, in order to demonstrate that a reasonable attempt was made to investigate. Since the law does not expect outsiders to attend hearings (the interviewer stands surrogate for evidence given by a member of the public), it is advisable to be accompanied by a witness.

People are often understandably reluctant to be interviewed for fear of causing someone to lose his job or even of reprisals.

A private householder ordered some new window frames to be fitted by someone whom he understood to be a private contractor. It was subsequently revealed that the contractor was actually an employee and that the frames had been stolen from his employer and fitted during working hours. The employee, however, visited the householder and told him to say nothing about the window frames or who had fitted them.

The best advice is to maximise the prospects of obtaining a statement by:

- Making it easy for the respondent. See him at home at his convenience.

- Emphasising that you need help, no one likes to refuse another person in need.

- Take particular care to avoid words like 'statement' and 'witness'.

- Introduce the person accompanying you simply as a colleague.

- Prepare thoroughly in order to obtain as much information as possible in one session.

- Be gentle but persistent. Respond to resistance with empathy then ask another question.

Incidentally, any indications of intimidation should be investigated as threats of any description are a legitimate management concern.

Interviewing children

No clear and definite rules exist on the involvement of children in disciplinary proceedings. As a guide, if a child is an important witness, an interview should be sought, though it is unlikely that the law would expect a child to attend a hearing. Children should be interviewed in the presence of another adult. A child should not be asked to sign a statement, the adult witness should do this as confirmation. Beware of undervaluing evidence just because it is a child who speaks. Equally, be mindful that children have been known to construct elaborate and convincing fantasies. So have some adults, cynics might add.

Handling the trade unions

Management have a clear right to conduct an investigation. As is often the case in industrial relations, however, it is the manner in which rights are exercised that is critical. The trade unions should be notified before interviews commence and informed of what they are likely to entail. Communication is the key to maintaining harmony. The worst thing that can happen is for a trade union to make the discovery by chance, usually via a distressed employee who wishes to lodge a grievance.

Key witnesses fall sick

A witness must be sufficiently fit and composed to respond to enquiries. Therefore, if a witness insists that he is too ill to be interviewed there is little that can be done. Nothing precludes trying to obtain a statement, however. For example, if the employee is immobilised, arrange transport or go and see him. If he is suffering from depression or anxiety write and suggest that worry over his employment may be contributing to his illness and that it might therefore be a good idea to resolve matters as quickly as possible. If the witness does agree to cooperate, before actually starting the interview check that he feels well enough to participate. Moreover, ensure this is recorded in the statement.

Where a witness dies or cannot be available for interview within a reasonable timescale, there may be no alternative but to proceed without their evidence. If so, reasonable account should be taken of the fact that the evidence is incomplete.

Distinguishing truth from falsehood

Detecting a false statement

As each piece of information emerges during an interview, ask yourself if it can logically be so. What, for example, is wrong with the following statement?

1. Q. Had you been to the café before?
   A. No.
2. Q. Were there prostitutes outside the café?
   A. Yes.
3. Q. Did they speak to you when you went in?
   A. No.

Surely the reference to the prostitutes is illogical? Prostitutes will normally proposition any potential client. The fact that they did not here suggests they knew the witness would not be interested in their services. In other words, the prostitutes recognised him and therefore his statement that he had never been to the café before was probably untrue.

Detecting collusion

Genuine accounts of the same phenomena always vary slightly. For instance, one person may describe a van as maroon, another will say it is red. Likewise, a fight viewed from different angles will result in discrepant, even conflicting, accounts of what took place depending on where the observer was standing.

Collusion on the other hand, produces identical statements reflecting the fact that the story is rehearsed. Statements can be tested by:

- Interviewing respondents separately.

- Asking questions going beyond the information contained in the statement.

- Asking questions out of sequence.

Those who rehearse must rely upon learning the story by heart. For example, whereas a genuine person will have little difficulty in remembering what happened third, fifth, or last, someone whose tale is rehearsed can usually only recount it chronologically.

Summary and checklist

- All witnesses must be interviewed.

208

- The purpose of an interview is to obtain a written account of events, known as a statement.

- Management have a right to question an employee about anything connected with his employment.

- An interview should be purposeful yet relaxed; serious yet empathetic.

- When interviewing, build rapport and lead gently into the subject with simple non-controversial questions.

- Use open questions to develop the story, ascertain dates, times and places.

- Silence forces the respondent to talk and helps him to remember things.

- As you listen, memorise key points.

- When the story is complete, summarise and repeat it back point by point. Then write it down.

- Conclude positively; check whether the respondent feels he has had a fair interview.

- A different technique is required to interview a hostile witness.

- A full investigation is necessary even where the employee confesses.

- Always try and obtain statements from children, members of the public and witnesses who fall sick.

- Notify the trade unions before commencing interviews.

- In evaluating statements ask yourself, 'can this logically be?'

Chapter Thirteen
Arranging a Disciplinary Hearing

Introduction

Having completed the investigation, two decisions are required, namely:

- whether to proceed to disciplinary action; and
- if so, on what basis?

This chapter advises on how to analyse and evaluate the results of an investigation and how to avoid legal pitfalls in wording allegations and in arranging a hearing.

Before becoming immersed in detail, however, a synoptic appraisal of the evidence is required to determine whether it really is a disciplinary case.

Is it a disciplinary case?

Effects of illness upon behaviour

Since investigations tend to focus upon what has happened rather than why, it is easy to overlook the possibility that illness may be affecting the employee's behaviour. If so, it is fruitless and unfair to continue with disciplinary proceedings. For example:

A headteacher complained about the behaviour and performance of one of his ancillary staff. On one occasion she was said to have reported for work on a Sunday. Recently she had poured custard into the children's drinking cups instead of on to their plates. More seriously she had been unable to locate the first-aid box when an emergency occurred in the playground.

When interviewed, the employee admitted she had momentarily forgotten the whereabouts of the first-aid box. She denied the other accusations.

This case underscores the point made earlier in this book about not becoming hypnotised by other people's definitions of reality. Although the headteacher viewed the employee's performance as a disciplinary matter, viewed with detachment, pouring custard into cups is an unlikely act of wilful misconduct or even carelessness, as is reporting for work on a Sunday. These taken together with the incident of the first-aid box suggest the employee is ill. She was, therefore, suspended on medical grounds and subsequently diagnosed as suffering from premature senile dementia. The employee had no recollection of her actions, hence her denial.

The next case also highlights the importance of reflecting upon the evidence and not rushing into setting up a disciplinary hearing.

A group of teachers complained that a female colleague had sexually enticed and humiliated a 14-year-old boy during a school trip.

The teacher was immediately suspended and an investigation ordered. The investigation found that the boy who was known to be infatuated with the teacher had been fondled by her, and she had made derogatory remarks about his sexual prowess.

Colleagues further reported seeing her consume white pills on the coach, and bursting into hysterical laughter periodically during the journey. She had also been seen sitting on a pavement swaying back and forth singing dirges. Her appearance was unkempt and she smelled as if she had been drinking gin. On the return journey another female member of staff sat beside her to prevent harm to the boy. The teacher then started caressing her colleague's hand.

Again, viewed dispassionately, the teacher's behaviour seems too public

211

and too extreme for it to be a simple case of misconduct. In fact, what began as an enquiry into allegations of serious misconduct plus drug and alcohol abuse, ended with the teacher being diagnosed as suffering from a schizophrenic illness and admitted to hospital.

Counselling as an alternative to disciplinary action

Even where misconduct has occurred, it is still necessary to decide whether disciplinary action is the best means of dealing with the problem.

A clerk who was bored and disaffected began to take odd days sick. Sometimes she failed to telephone by the stipulated time and her work had usually been left in a mess.

The aim of a counselling interview is to avoid disciplinary action by addressing the underlying problem and by devising a positive approach to dealing with it. It emerged here that the deterioration in performance stemmed from boredom and more particularly from perceived lack of career prospects. Counselling enabled the clerk to clarify her aspirations and to develop a career and training plan whereas disciplinary action might have destroyed any prospect of motivating the employee.

A teacher was promoted to a job of coordinator of a special unit. Within six months the staff of the unit lodged a grievance against him. An investigation was held which established that relations between the coordinator and his staff had broken down. The coordinator was perceived as a rigid authoritarian and staff felt unable to work with him.

Ostensibly a dismissal case, in reality an unwise appointment as the teacher had been an exemplary employee until becoming coordinator. When counselled, he said that he had felt unhappy and lacked confidence as a manager which made him appear coercive and inflexible. The problem was resolved by re-training and transferring the employee.

A management interview as an alternative to disciplinary action

Where the evidence is weak or where a case is serious but not sufficiently so to pursue to disciplinary action, a management interview can be held instead. The purpose of a management interview is to issue an informal warning. Its value is that:

- it can pave the way to disciplinary action;
- there are no rights of appeal; and
- there is no time limit.

It is advisable to confirm a management interview in writing. Written confirmation is proof of a reasonable effort to resolve problems informally and it ensures that the employee was well aware of how his conduct or performance was viewed long before disciplinary proceedings were enacted.

Analysing the evidence

Where there is a disciplinary case to answer the next stages are:

- to identify the concerns emanating from the investigation;
- to decide which of these to pursue to disciplinary action; and
- to translate them into specific allegations.

Identifying concerns

It was said in Chapter Ten that all investigations begin with a concern over an employee's conduct or performance. Investigations typically substantiate, modify or add to the original concerns. An analysis of the evidence is therefore required to identify the basis of a disciplinary case.

The analysis must be systematic otherwise something important may be missed. A good method is to read through all the statements and other evidence highlighting potential disciplinary issues. Aim to level as many accusations as possible without appearing frivolous or vindictive. Even at this early stage however, selectivity is recommended by ignoring trivial or inadequately supported issues.

Selecting accusations

Having completed an initial appraisal of the evidence, next examine each of the concerns identified in more detail and decide which to pursue to disciplinary action. Concentrate on issues which are:

- serious;
- tangible;
- adequately corroborated;

- recent; and

- indefensible, ie carrying minimum risk of a successful plea of mitigation.

The more fully each of these five criteria is met, the stronger the case. For example, of the following concerns which once emanated from an enquiry into dishonesty, which would you concentrate upon?

- Held a Christmas party three years ago despite an instruction that office parties were banned.

- Failed to observe financial regulations when inviting tenders for a £5 million woodcutting machine.

- Failed to act after seeing company property being loaded into a private car.

- Sold eggs to other staff contrary to regulations forbidding employees to use their jobs for private gain.

The first accusation is relatively trivial and intangible. Indeed, it would probably be unfair to pursue it after three years as memories fade and staff move on.

The fourth allegation, selling eggs, would sound ludicrous at a hearing and, moreover, distract attention from accusations two and three which are potentially serious disciplinary matters. In particular, failure to observe financial regulations is extremely serious, and not only that but also the easiest to prove as it will probably be supported by documentary evidence. Even if the incident occurred two to three years ago, since it potentially involves a serious fraud it is still a valid concern. Furthermore, since the rules are strict and well publicised, the likelihood of a plea in mitigation being accepted is low.

Specifying accusations

It is essential that accusations are expressed:

- precisely; and

- in plain English.

An employee must know exactly what he is accused of. Terms such as 'Poor performance' or 'Lateness' on their own are too vague. The accusation must indicate exactly what it is about the employee's performance or timekeeping which is unsatisfactory.

Poor performance, that is, consistent failure to achieve sales targets over the last 18 months.

Poor timekeeping, that is, lateness on 12 occasions in the last month.

Terminology should be used carefully. Only accuse someone of 'incapability' if there is evidence that the employee is incapable. If what you really mean is poor performance, say so.

Avoid circumlocution or legalistic language. These tend to produce confusion where clarity is critical. Terms like 'hereafter', 'aforeto' and 'hereinsaid' are more likely to indicate inexperience on the part of the writer than to impress. Accusations phrased as 'Did remove the cash box without authorisation instant' jar the eye and sound ridiculous. What does 'instant' mean? It is much simpler and clearer to say: 'Unauthorised removal of the cash box'.

Making the most of the evidence

Accusations should be set out in a way that conveys maximum impact. For instance, the statement:

- Unauthorised absence from work between 26 and 30 August and September 4 to September 8.

makes less impression than:

- Unauthorised absence from work between 26 and 30 August for five days.

- Unauthorised absence from work from September 4 to September 8 for five days.

Both sets of accusations contain the same information but the second has more impact than the first. This is because it is immediately apparent from the second set of allegations that the employee has been absent without permission not once but twice, and for a total of ten days within a short space of time. In the first example, the reader has to work this out; by making his task easier you also help yourself.

The reason for listing accusations separately is to prevent losing the whole case if one part is disproved. Furthermore, a list of accusations helps the chairperson to steer the hearing and makes it more difficult for the employee to evade issues by forcing him to answer the whole case, bit by bit.

Accusations should be listed systematically either in chronological order or in descending order of seriousness, whichever makes the greatest impact.

Selecting and specifying accusations; a worked example

The process of identifying concerns and framing allegations can best be illustrated by the following extract from a witness's statement:

1. Most of the staff got fed up with Mr Stapleton. *Whenever there was a problem he didn't want to know.* We started going to his office in pairs, one of us would go round the back to stop him slipping out which he regularly did if there was a problem.

2. *Whenever Mr Stapleton was on the rota to work evening duty with me he used to disappear down to the pub.* When I said to him I did not know what view the authority would take of this he asked me if I wanted to be third in charge or not. He said the experience of being in sole charge would look good on my CV. I am on evening rota with Mr Stapleton twice a week and on each of these occasions since January 1989 he has left the site to visit the pub.

3. *One night about six months ago, Mr Stapleton left Mrs Curry, a welfare assistant, to deal with one of the girls in care, Amanda Jenkins who was crying with pain. The nurse had refused to see her (she never took any notice of Mr Stapleton). After that he just went back to bed. The girl had her appendix out two days later.*

4. Not many people like working here. A lot of good staff have left over the last three or four years. *There were no schemes of work for the children, no educational policy, no record books kept by staff, and the log book has not been completed for two years.* Mr Stapleton seemed to have favourites among the staff, if you were well in with him he was generally quite pleasant ...

The sections in italics identify the potential disciplinary concerns. Note how the investigator has already exercised some selectivity, for example, the reference to favouritism at the end of the statement has been ignored as there is no concrete evidence to substantiate it.

The next step is to examine the specific concerns to consider which to pursue to disciplinary action. The first issue, evading staff, is probably the least tangible of the list but it is still significant especially if corroborated by other staff.

Visiting a public house while on duty is a clear breach of contract and all the more reprehensible because of the employee's position of trust. The incident concerning the child who was ill during the night represents both a serious failure to fulfil the duty of *in loco parentis*, and a failure to deal with the school nurse subsequently.

Allegations concerning schemes of work and so forth are serious and easy to substantiate. Either these exist or they do not. The same applies to the log book. Either it has been kept properly or it has not.

The concerns must then be translated into allegations as follows:

- Visiting a public house while on duty.

- Failing to exercise proper care over Amanda Jenkins.

- Failure to deal appropriately with the conduct of the school nurse following the incident with Amanda Jenkins.

- Failure to provide academic leadership in that:
    — no schemes of work exist;
    — there is no educational policy within the school;
    — no staff records are maintained; and
    — staff are inadequately supported.

- Failure to maintain the school log book.

Calling an employee to a disciplinary hearing

It cannot be over-emphasised that cases can be lost at a tribunal if proper procedures are not followed. It is therefore essential to pay meticulous attention to detail in composing letters. In particular, always make doubly sure that:

- The employee knows that it is a disciplinary hearing to which he is being called.

- That he knows in advance exactly what the allegations are, and, of his rights to representation.

- That the allegations reflect the evidence.

The employee must receive written notice of a hearing. This must clearly indicate the status of the meeting and also incorporate the following information:

1. The date, time and place of the hearing.
2. The allegations.
3. Rights to trade union representation.

A specimen letter is set out below:

Dear

① → You are instructed to attend a disciplinary hearing on 4 February in the works manager's office at 2.00 pm.

② → The hearing will be held in accordance with the company's agreed disciplinary procedure and you will be required to respond to the following allegations:

217

   a.   Unauthorised removal of a portable welding kit.

   b.   Behaving abusively towards a security officer.

③ →   You are entitled to be accompanied to the hearing by either your trade union representative or a colleague.

   Yours sincerely

The time and place of the hearing may seem obvious as indeed they are. However, they can assume considerable importance if the employee fails to attend the hearing and subsequently claims he was not told of the venue or the time at which he should have attended.

All of the allegations must be set out in the letter. Moreover, these must be consistent with management's case. In other words, it is inadmissable to allege unauthorised removal then, at the hearing, accuse the employee of theft.

Even though the employee is well aware of his rights to representation they must, nevertheless, be stated in the letter. There is no substitute for written proof that procedures have been followed.

If the employee is in work, the letter is best delivered in person by the line manager. If not, hand delivery to the last known address is the safest method of conveyance in which case the letter should be marked 'Hand delivered'. If this is impracticable, recorded delivery is the next best alternative.

Accompanying documentation

It is advisable to give the employee copies of all statements and other documentary evidence to ensure that he knows the case against him. It is weak to 'reserve' part of your case for a surprise attack at the hearing. If a proper investigation has taken place, there should be nothing more to add. Besides, it is not unusual for an employee, on seeing the evidence, to resign!

Notice required for a hearing

No rules govern the length of notice required for hearing. As a guide, it should be sufficient to enable the employee to:

- arrange trade union representation;

- assimilate management's evidence; and

- prepare a defence.

It is imperative that the employee has reasonable time in which to study the evidence and prepare his own case. If suspended, he should be granted access (if necessary under supervision) to whatever papers, diaries or other sources he requires.

Equally, there should be no undue delay as the law requires disciplinary proceedings to be expedited quickly. Where procedures specify that a particular manager should hear the case, and where this would delay the hearing unreasonably (eg because of illness or extended holiday commitments), it is acceptable for an equal ranking or more senior manager to hear the case.

Employees required as witnesses can be instructed to attend the hearing. Due account should be taken of holiday commitments and so forth as the absence of a key witness could lead to unfairness.

It is reasonable to accommodate the commitments of trade union representatives provided these are not used as delaying tactics. If procrastination occurs, it is permissible to set a date for a hearing and leave it to the trade unions to organise representation. Management's obligation is to inform the employee of his rights to such representation, not to arrange it for him. It is appreciated, however, that in many organisations, this would lead to industrial action. If so, the best advice is to be patient and to be seen to be reasonable by offering alternative dates and times. If this fails, give the trade union at least one further opportunity to cooperate by saying something like 'If this goes on, I am going to have to set a date anyway'.

Employee fails to attend

Note that the letter calling the employee to the hearing is an instruction and not a request. If the employee fails to attend, two options exist:

- to conduct the hearing in his absence; or

- to arrange another hearing and to add a further allegation.

The second option is the safer because it gives the employee an opportunity to explain if something genuinely prevented his attendance. It also serves to demonstrate that management have acted reasonably in exercising patience and in giving the employee full opportunity to put his case. If levied, the additional allegation should read 'Failure to comply with an instruction to attend a disciplinary hearing'. It is stressed that the case must be considered *in toto*. In other words, it would be unfair to administer a final warning for the original allegations and then convene another hearing and dismiss the employee for failing to attend the first.

Where an employee has already failed to attend a management interview or has a bad record, the first option may be justified. If so, the letter calling the employee to the hearing should state that if he fails to attend, the hearing will be held in his absence. If dismissal is a possible outcome, this should be stated.

Summary and checklist

- Having completed the investigation the next task is to decide whether disciplinary action is appropriate, and, if so, on what basis.

- Where a case exists, an analysis of the evidence is required to identify specific allegations.

- Allegations must be precise and expressed in plain English.

- Bring as many allegations as possible but concentrate on the most serious and the easiest to prove.

- The employee must be notified of the hearing in writing.

- The letter should specify the date, time and place of the hearing; the allegations; and rights to representation.

- The employee should receive copies of all statements and other documentary evidence.

- Disciplinary proceedings must be expedited promptly. Equally, the employee must be allowed reasonable time to prepare his case.

- If the employee fails to attend the hearing, it can be conducted in his absence.

Chapter Fourteen
Preparing to Present a Case

Introduction

Although brilliant advocacy cannot redeem a poor investigation, a good case can be ruined by a poor presentation. Furthermore, although hearings and tribunals must always be conducted impartially, chairpersons can be influenced for good or ill by both the style of the presentation itself, and not least the manner and bearing of the presenter. This chapter advises on how to make an effective presentation, and, on how to secure maximum psychological advantage in doing so.

The golden rules of advocacy

These are:

- Clarity.
- Simplicity.
- Brevity.
- Liveliness.
- Integrity.
- Humility.

It is easy for presenters, themselves fully briefed, to forget that the chairperson is hearing the evidence for the first time and may be unfamiliar with background details and technicalities. *Clarity* is achieved by assuming no knowledge on the part of those hearing the case. Moreover, presentations should be edited to eliminate needless repetition and superfluous material.

Clarity also applies to documentary evidence. Make the chairperson's task easy by ensuring that all material is clear, key points are highlighted and written explanations accompany tables or other non-textual data. Use flip chart presentations and other visual aids where these facilitate explanation and understanding. Furthermore, it is essential to be well organised and not engender impatience by fumbling for papers, missing parts of the case, presenting erroneous information and so forth.

Simplicity is the midwife of clarity. Speak as you would to a child. Far from sounding condescending, you will come across as having a good grasp of the case. In dealing with fraud, for example, rather than present a complicated sheet of accounts, summarise the information in a way that someone unfamiliar with accounting terms and conventions can understand. For example:

- In: £14,000

- Out: £12,500

- *Discrepancy* £1,500

Although this is an over-simplification, it does show how the reader's attention is immediately drawn to the nub of the case, ie a significant and unexplained shortfall in the accounts. The full balance sheet or other source data should always be made available. These are best presented in separate appendices.

Brevity is always appreciated by those whose duty it is to listen. It is a mistake to believe that your case will be bolstered by expounding upon every issue regardless of its relevance. Keep it as short as possible. In particular, never waste time in pursuing pointless arguments or in challenging the other side down to the last detail.

Liveliness of presentation helps retain the listener's attention. At very least, prevent attention from wandering by maintaining eye contact with the chairperson and by varying your tone and pace. A little humour (provided it is carefully controlled) also helps. Essentially the presenter is telling a story; try therefore to build a little interest and excitement. Even where the facts are fairly pedestrian, try nonetheless to make the story as engaging as possible. Instead of saying:

On 24 November an investigation commenced into allegations of malpractice and misappropriation at North Depot following the discovery of a trade card which bore a similar address to the manager's . . .;

begin with:

Chair, this investigation was sparked by a chance discovery. An auditor on a routine visit to the depot noticed that one of the supplier's trade cards happened to have a similar address to the manager. Curiosity turned to suspicion when . . .

In the first example, the presenter is simply relating the facts of the case. While this is acceptable, in the second example we see how the same facts are presented in a much more engaging manner as the presenter has used his material to weave an interesting and lucid story. This does not imply distorting or exaggerating the facts of the case; it means expending thought and effort in trying to make the listener's task easy and interesting.

The task of the presenter is to assist the chairperson, not to win at all costs. Never misrepresent the facts to fit the case, withhold information, or allow anyone else to do so. A reputation for *integrity* in the eyes of colleagues, employees and the trade unions is worth more in the long run than winning a dubious case which might in any event be overturned later.

Avoid courtroom mannerisms, be natural, courteous and appropriately deferential. A little *humility* in addressing the chair is not only pleasant to he who receives it, it actually conveys an impression of professionalism and confidence. The pompous barrister manqué generally achieves the opposite. Declarations such as 'Chairman, in all my 20 years as manager, I have never seen such complete incompetence', are more likely to lose support than win it, even if they are true. Neither does passing moral judgements or denigrating employees. For instance, 'Mr Chairman, you see before you someone whom this organisation rescued from the scrap-heap. That same person, whom this organisation rescued from the dole queue has repaid us with deceit and dishonesty . . .'. Few people are impressed by an emotional tirade based on a third rate imitation of some television lawyer. A sound case requires no embellishment.

Preparing a script

The most common methods are to:

- speak from memory;

- write out a script; or

- make notes of key points.

The first option has little to recommend it. It is easy to omit an important point, and seeking permission to go back to an earlier stage of the process makes a poor impression. Worse, should your memory fail under the stress of the hearing, you may discredit yourself by being unable to continue at all.

Writing out a script in full is probably the safest method especially for the inexperienced. Beware, however, of reciting it parrot-fashion. Blank verse is a most effective means of preventing a presentation from degenerating into a toneless mumble. For example:

Chairman,
I will bring evidence
to show
That Mr Jones
Has consistently
Failed
To carry out
his duties, and responsibilities.

Poetic ability is unimportant as the purpose of this technique is to ensure that key points receive emphasis. Whenever possible, arrange for the script to be typed, generously spaced. It is time-consuming but well worth the effort, especially if it is your first case. You will be able to speak without worrying about being unable to read your own handwriting or translating your notes into speech or losing your place at a critical moment.

A set of well-produced notes is a good compromise. The level of detail is a matter of personal preference. As a guide, however, notes should contain:

- All the points to be raised.

- Sufficient detail to enable background information to be recalled.

- Elaborate signposting.

For example, a case prepared in note form might read:

1. Explain case concerns <u>failure to carry out responsibilities</u>.
2. Produce <u>job description</u> and draw attention to clauses highlighted.

Notes should be regarded as essentially a condensed version of a full script. Signposting such as underlining or headings will help prevent key points from being missed and help you regain your place should you be distracted. Cards are easier to organise than paper and cause less distraction through rustling.

Getting started

It is a waste of time to begin composing until you have all the information to hand and organised. A good way of mastering the issues is to begin by summarising the case and then developing each major point on separate sheets or cards.

Editing the presentation

Remember, once you are in a hearing, your notes or script are all you have to rely upon. Redrafting will be worth the effort. The best way of testing a presentation is to read it aloud and mark any flaws as you go. Do not be dismayed if you find it necessary to repeat the process several times. Amateurs, it is said, rehearse until they have got it right; professionals until they cannot get it wrong. Aim to emulate the latter.

Should I call witnesses?

In law, you are not obliged to call witnesses but if you do, you stand or fall by what they say. A decision must, therefore, be made between the potential gain of promoting the case versus the risk of damaging it as a result of a poor witness. The risk can be significantly reduced, however, by preparation. Witnesses are naturally apprehensive, ensure therefore that they understand:

- The nature of the hearing and how it will be conducted.

- The questions you intend to put and how to answer.

- The purpose of cross-examination and how to respond.

- How to conduct themselves generally while giving evidence.

Witnesses should be coached to speak clearly, audibly and confidently. Equally, they should be discouraged, firmly if necessary, from exaggeration, irrelevance or departing from the question. There is nothing dishonest about preparing a witness; it is a sensible way of ensuring that the hearing proceeds smoothly, with minimum distress, and that a fair decision results.

How to present a case

A most effective method is to:

- begin by telling the chair what you intend to tell him;

- tell him; and then

- tell him what you have already told him.

These three stages are known respectively as:

1. Opening the case.
2. Presenting the evidence in detail.
3. Summing up.

We now examine each of these in detail.

Opening a case

The opening of a case should contain only what is essential to draw the chairperson's attention to the issues he must consider. Normally this entails:

- stating the allegations,
- followed by a very brief summary of the evidence; and
- a very brief summary of the conclusions.

Here is an example of a good opening:

> During the hearing I will bring evidence to substantiate two allegations, namely that Mr Twist removed a portable welding kit from the premises without permission, and that when challenged, he was abusive towards a security officer.
>
> Witnesses will describe Mr Twist's quite unacceptable behaviour towards the security guard. Furthermore, my evidence will show that there is no dispute that the kit was removed by Mr Twist, and that strict and well-publicised rules exist that unauthorised removal is regarded as gross misconduct and, therefore, a dismissable offence.

In two succinct paragraphs the chairperson is told to listen for two allegations, what those allegations are and the approach the presenter intends to take. That is, he confidently suggests that the facts concerning the most serious element of the case are irrefutable and that the case is sound because the rules concerning removal of the kits have been properly communicated. This can hardly fail to make a good impression.

Note also that in the second paragraph, the order in which the allegations are referred to is reversed. This is an example of what was said earlier about creating impact and weaving together an effective presentation. While it would have been acceptable simply to address the allegations in chronological order, a much sharper focus is achieved by this manner of presentation. Not only does it suggest that the presenter has mastered the case, it increases the likelihood of a satisfactory outcome by ensuring that the chair understands that the major issue is not that Mr

Twist was abusive, though this forms part of the case, but that he is guilty of gross misconduct by removing a welding kit.

Presenting a case in detail

The next step is to present evidence in detail. The presentation must contain all the relevant evidence and enough background information for the chairperson to understand the case. Incidentally, a useful tip for presenters is that it is better to reveal evidence adverse to your case at this stage than to wait for the other side to expose it in cross-examination later.

Disciplinary hearings are not courts of law and, therefore, considerable flexibility extends to the way in which a case is presented — provided the rules of natural justice are observed. The most common approach is for the presenter to open the case, describe the background and then call witnesses to relate the main parts of the evidence. This is by no means obligatory, however. An alternative is for the presenter to give the evidence with minimal reliance upon witnesses. The degree of reliance upon witnesses depends upon the nature of the evidence, the dependability of the witnesses and the extent to which the facts of the case are in dispute.

The first approach is the most common because a first-hand account usually has more impact and credibility than one that is second- or even third-hand. The disadvantage of course is that the presenter has less control because of the reliance upon witnesses. A good compromise is for the presenter to narrate most of the case, calling witnesses to recount key passages of the evidence.

Controlling witnesses

It is the presenter's responsibility to guide and control the witness. The witness who is merely asked to tell his story or give his evidence, usually confuses everyone else and then lapses into confusion himself. Take him up to the essential points and, if necessary, interrupt to keep his account precise and chronological. For example:

Presenter: Portable welding kits are stored on the loading bay. Security is tight and enforced by strict rules because they are not only expensive, but very handy for carrying out work on cars and other DIY jobs. They cost £7,000 each.

I would now like to call Mr Spanner the loading bay supervisor.

Mr Spanner, would you explain to the chair how the welding kit was discovered missing?

Witness: Er yes, well, last Thursday night I was doing the usual stock check and I saw one of the kits wasn't there.

Presenter: What did you do then?

Witness: I immediately reported it to the depot manager.

Presenter: Can you tell us why you did that?

Witness: Because security over kits is very strict. We have to report it straight away if any go missing.

Presenter Thank you. I would now like to call Mr Driver, the depot manager.

Mr Driver, you have heard what Mr Spanner has just said, about security and reporting that a kit was missing. Is it correct?

Witness: Yes.

Presenter: Would you please tell the chair what happened after Mr Spanner reported that the kit was missing?

Witness: I informed security who locked the gates. We then called everyone on site together and said we wanted to examine the boot of everyone's car.

Note how questions are used to break up the story so that the sequence of events can be readily understood. This is particularly important when dealing with a complex case. It is better to keep the witness to the point by asking three or four specific questions than to leave him with one very general one.

Leading questions and how to avoid them

A leading question is one which suggests the answer to the witness. Court proceedings largely forbid the asking of leading questions. Although disciplinary procedures are not so strictly regulated, leading questions should, nonetheless, be avoided where possible. For instance, in the case of welding kits, a leading question would be to ask the security guard 'Was Mr Bungle abusive towards you?'

Avoiding a leading question usually entails asking a series of questions. For example:

Presenter: What are the rules concerning suspected theft?

Guard: The gates are locked immediately and all employees and their belongings must be searched.

Presenter: Did you search Mr Twist?

Guard:	I tried to, yes.
Presenter:	What happened?
Guard:	He told me to 'f... off'.
Presenter:	I see, what happened after that?
Guard:	I said 'I must examine the boot of your car'.
Presenter:	What did Mr Twist do then?
Guard:	He stepped in front of me, pushed me away and said 'Naff off'.

When examining witnesses, restrain yourself from repeating everything the witness has said. Far from adding emphasis it tends to become tedious and irritating.

Cross-examination

Each side has the opportunity to question the other's case. This is known as cross-examination. It is emphasised that the aim of cross-examination is not to discover anything new but either to promote your own case or to weaken the other side's. The golden rule of cross-examination, and indeed of any part of formal proceedings is *never ask a question to which you do not already know the answer.*

The dangers of forgetting this fundamental precept are illustrated by the next case which concerned two Council employees dismissed for being in a public house on Christmas Eve when they should have been gritting roads. Here is how the trade union representative cross-examined the landlord of the pub at the industrial tribunal:

1. Q. What night was it you claimed to have seen my members in your pub?
   A. Christmas Eve.
2. Q. What time was that?
   A. About nine o'clock.
3. Q. Tell me, was the pub empty that night?
   A. No, it was extremely busy.
4. Q. Is the pub brightly lit?
   A. No, it has subdued lighting.
5. Q. Almost dark in fact?
   A. Yes.
6. Q. Then how can you be certain it was my members you saw?
   A. Because they were the only people wearing fluorescent jackets.

Question 6. might aptly be described as a question too many. Had the trade union official confined himself to the preceding five, he might have succeeded in creating some doubt as to the employees' identity. Alas, by asking a question to which he did not know the answer, not only did he destroy what he had built, worse, he delivered his members to a grateful management.

Should I cross-examine?

Effective cross-examination requires skill and practice. Furthermore, it is a risky process because although you know what the answer should be, you cannot predict whether the witness will answer the question put or control what he says. The first question a presenter should therefore ask himself is, need I cross-examine at all? If a witness has said nothing which harms your case, why question him and take the risk of him saying something which will?

To reduce the risk, a cross-examination should always be as short as possible. Moreover, it should always be purposeful and directed to significant points. Questions should be prepared beforehand though others may be added, depending on evidence given by the employee's side. The safest form of cross-examination is that based on irrefutable evidence notably correspondence or other documents:

1. Q. Mr Bungle, did you say in your statement you were unaware of the financial regulations?
   A. Yes.
2. Q. Your words were 'There were no proper rules'.
   A. Yes.
3. Q. Would you look at this memo please; is this your handwriting?
   A. Yes.
4. Q. Would you read the last line aloud please?
   A. 'If anyone finds out about this, there will be hell to pay.'

Re-examination

It is customary for respective parties to re-examine witnesses after cross-examination. The purpose of re-examination is to put answers given in the cross-examination in proper perspective. New evidence cannot be introduced. An effective re-examination requires careful observation of the evidence given in cross-examination, and, effective note taking. Never re-examine merely for the sake of it; direct your attention to matters which have emerged to your disadvantage in the cross-examination. For example, a teacher accused of 'butting' a child argued that he had only tapped her head. The school nurse was cross-examined as follows:

1. Q. Did you examine the child?
    A. Yes.
2. Q. Did you see any signs of bruising on her head?
    A. No.

Then the re-examination:

1. Q. How soon after the accident did you examine the girl?
    A. Three weeks.

Summing up

At the end of the hearing, each side summarises its case. The summary serves the same purpose as the opening, ie to draw the chairperson's attention to the major issues. No new evidence can be introduced. The same words can be used in the summing up as in the introduction. Modifications may be necessary as a result of the hearing, though if the investigation has been sound, summary and introduction will be interchangeable. In other words, there will have been no surprises at the hearing.

It is the chairperson's responsibility to decide the penalty. Offering an opinion is poor style; it may even be resented. A more polished way of rounding off is to ask one or two questions. For instance, a case concerning wilful violation of safety regulations might end with:

Chair, in concluding this presentation I would ask you to consider two questions. First how many people might have been killed or injured as a consequence of this wilful disregard of simple, basic instructions?

Second, I would ask you to consider whether you can continue to have trust and confidence in Mr —— having heard what little regard he has shown for the safety of his colleagues?

Be careful where the employee is repentant, or where there are genuine mitigating circumstances as this tactic may make you appear pugnacious. In these circumstances questions should be carefully prefaced, for example 'Chair, it is evident that Mr —— now understands how foolishly he has behaved. At the same time I ask you to consider what might have happened had his act of carelessness not been discovered?' If in doubt, leave the questions out.

Summary and checklist

*   The best way to present a case is:
    — tell the chair what you intend to say;

- say it;
- tell him what you have said.

- Clarity, simplicity, brevity, liveliness, integrity and humility are the most important rules of advocacy.

- Rehearse your presentation at least once and be prepared to redraft it several times if necessary.

- Avoid pomposity and making personal attacks.

- You are not obliged to call witnesses, but if you do, you stand or fall by what they say, therefore prepare them.

- Guide a witness through his story or evidence.

- The purpose of cross-examination is either to emphasise your own case or weaken your opponent's.

- The purpose of re-examination is to set your evidence in perspective.

- Both cross-examination and re-examination are risky processes to be used only if a witness has said something which harms your case. Keep both short and to the point.

- Round off a case by asking one or two questions.

Chapter Fifteen
Holding a Disciplinary Hearing

Introduction

It was noted in Chapter One that the purposes of a disciplinary hearing are to decide:

- whether reasonable grounds exist for belief in the employee's guilt; and

- the penalty, if any.

Provided the rules of natural justice are observed, employers have considerable flexibility in deciding how to conduct proceedings. A suitable procedure for a disciplinary hearing is set out below.

Model procedure for conducting a disciplinary hearing

1. The chairperson shall introduce everyone present.
2. The chairperson shall explain the procedure.
3. Management shall present their case and may call witnesses.
4. The employee or his representatives may cross-examine management and any witnesses.
5. Management may re-examine witnesses.
6. The employee or his representatives present their case and may call witnesses.
7. Management may cross-examine the employee or his representatives and any witnesses.
8. The employee or his representatives may re-examine any witnesses.
9. The chairperson may ask questions of either side.
10. Management sum up.
11. The employee or his representatives sum up.
12. Both sides shall withdraw.

Responsibilities of the chairperson

These are to ensure that the hearing is conducted in an orderly manner and that natural justice is observed. A disciplinary hearing is usually an unpleasant experience for all participants. A further responsibility of the chairperson therefore, is to minimise distress.

Organising a hearing

Ensure that both parties have separate waiting facilities, if possible away from curious eyes. Treat trade union representatives with the same courtesy and consideration that you would wish for yourself.

At the commencement of proceedings, both sides should be called into the room simultaneously. It is imperative that the chairperson is not seen conferring with any member of the management side immediately prior to the hearing as this could be interpreted as showing bias. If this is unavoidable, for instance if an urgent matter unconnected with the hearing arises, this should be explained to both sides before starting the hearing. If an objection is raised, the manager concerned may offer to stand down, to allow another manager to hear the case. It is advisable to make the offer and ensure that it is recorded. Usually the employee's side will waive it.

Ensure that you will not be disturbed. A hearing may take place round a table or in easy chairs. It is customary for both sides to be physically separate, usually by sitting at opposite sides of the table or room. It is useful if the respective presenters sit nearest to the chairperson followed by key witnesses. Alternatively witnesses may be called as required. Serving coffee is usually appreciated and helps lower tension. Open simply by saying 'We are in a disciplinary hearing: I shall begin by introducing everyone'.

Introductions are not only polite, they are also a subtle means of taking charge. Next, explain the procedure and check that it is acceptable to the employee's side. Polished courtesy from the chairperson encourages others to reciprocate. For example, at each stage ask the presenter if he is ready to begin and thank him at the end.

Controlling the hearing

It is the chairperson's responsibility to ensure that order is maintained and everyone is kept to the point. Inexperienced advocates sometimes have difficulty in framing questions when cross-examining and therefore lapse into repetition or sidetracking. If this happens intercede gently by asking 'Is this a question?' Similarly, at the summing-up stage it may be necessary to stop someone from going through the whole case again.

Interruptions from the chair, however, must never violate the rules of natural justice. It is one thing to cut short a rambling witness, another to prevent him from being heard. The best advice is to err on the side of caution. Better to lose half an hour listening to a protracted tale than to have a judgement overturned on the grounds that the employee was denied the opportunity to defend himself.

Where an employee is unrepresented or represented by someone inexperienced, the chairperson should make reasonable efforts to assist them with the presentation of their case. Likewise the chairperson can agree to requests from the employee's side to vary the procedure providing this does not prevent management's case from being properly heard. Again, the best advice in dealing with procedural matters is to exercise discretion in favour of the employee.

Common defence strategies

When management's case is strong, experienced trade union representatives will often try and detract attention from it. It is important, therefore, that both those hearing cases and those presenting them are aware of the five commonest tactics and how to counter them.

Attacking management

This is the most common tactic consisting of loud denunciations accompanied by table banging and other similar theatrical effects. For example:

- 'The whole handling of this case is appalling.'

- 'It is disgraceful that my member should have to sit here and listen to this.'

- 'I have serious concerns about the role of management in all this.'

- 'It should be management who are disciplined, not my member.'

- 'Management have spied on my member, their behaviour is disgusting.'

- 'My member is being victimised by a vindictive management.'

Do not be put off by words like 'disgusting', 'appalling' and 'victimisation'. Once you have heard the same trade union official use the same phrases at every disciplinary hearing, you will find that they lose their impact. It is best to ignore these attacks until summing up. At that stage, point out that no one has actually challenged the facts of the case and that nothing has been said that actually changes anything.

A plea in mitigation

Beware the trade union representative who interrupts at the beginning of the hearing and says 'Chair, here is a case where the facts are not in dispute'. Far from conceding defeat, he may be just about to win. This is because he will then say 'So perhaps I could just say a few words on behalf of my member'. The chairperson nods sympathetically and this follows:

> Thank you, Chair. I would just like to say that Mr Jones is an honest, hard-working man. He has five children and a wife who is an invalid. All his life has been a struggle to keep his family together and to stop his children being taken into care. They depend on him as father and sole provider. At 53, he will never get another job. For the sake of a momentary lapse, this simple and dignified working man will have to go home, virtually on Christmas Eve, and tell his family that he has lost his job. Chair, I'm asking you, not just for Mr Jones, but for his family, to use your power to spare him that.

This technique works by diverting attention from the employee's misconduct and by seeking to arouse sympathy by emphasising his personal plight. The nearest we come to the employee's conduct is the reference to a 'momentary lapse'. We are not enlightened to the fact that this so-called lapse involved selling hundreds of pounds' worth of company property to a builders' merchant.

Pleas like this tend to be construed in language that would almost certainly guarantee prosecution under the Trades Description Act. For 'momentary lapse' or 'unfortunate discretion' read 'evidence to support a single act of gross misconduct'. 'Foolish action' on the other hand means offences committed over many years. Christmas Eve runs from August while between January and July it is approaching the holidays. A single person is invariably 'lonely'; if divorced 'traumatised and lonely'. If all else fails he will be 'under great pressure or stressed'. Anyone aged over 35 will certainly never work again. Note also how the chairperson has been elevated to the status of Roman Emperor '... use your power to spare him ...'

This is not to trivialise pleas in mitigation. The chairperson must listen to and consider whatever the employee or his representative wishes to say. Here, however, the trade union representative is seeking to make a one-sided presentation. If chairing a hearing, reply that in the interests of justice and clarity, the whole case should be put. If presenting a case, interject and insist upon being heard.

Bluff

Beware the trade union representative who arrives armed with rule books, masses of notes, copies of memos and directives. It is usually a ploy to undermine the presenter's confidence and to discourage him from prosecuting with full vigour by suggesting the possibility of a disastrous flaw in management's case. Another variation of this tactic is the triumphant look, and appearing to fish for a piece of paper just as you are making a point. There is little that can be done about this form of psychological warfare except to remember this is one game both sides can play.

Sowing confusion

> Said a judge to a barrister "You really are confusing this case terribly." The barrister replied "I thank you Sir."

As this anecdote suggests, another way of countering a thorough and well-documented case is to dwell upon irrelevancies or deliberately to misunderstand the issue:

An employee broke into his employer's garage over the weekend and drove off with a car to take his girlfriend out. At the hearing, the trade union representative focused upon the fact that there were no rules about the use of company vehicles for private purposes.

Management insisted there were indeed regulations and the hearing was adjourned while filing cabinets were searched and drawers turned out in a frantic effort to produce them.

So successful was the trade union representative in setting this hare running, that dismissal was commuted to a final warning. No one paused to question what the existence or otherwise of these rules had to do with breaking into premises.

Where multiple accusations are involved, a variation of this tactic is to focus upon the least serious or the weakest. For example, a joiner disciplined principally for poor attendance, was also accused of leaving the site half an hour early. His trade union representative focused exclusively upon the latter arguing that the employee had gone only ten minutes early; that the depot clock was wrong; management were lying and so forth. The fact that the joiner had had 186 days absence in the last year was forgotten.

If chairing a hearing, allow the trade union representative to make his point as it is important that he is seen to be defending his member. Intervene only if it is clear that the whole case is becoming hopelessly sidetracked. If presenting a case, be sure when summing up to recapitulate and emphasise the substantive issues.

Minimisation

This tactic aims to reduce the disciplinary penalty by sowing doubt over the degree of misconduct. For example, a library porter accused of throwing a teenager's radio into a wastepaper bin maintained that he had 'placed' it there.

This is where a thorough investigation pays. Remember, it is not only *what* a witness knows that is important but *how* he comes to know it. For instance, it is insufficient simply to record merely that a witness saw someone throw a radio in a wastepaper bin. What did he actually do and say? Did he seem angry and if so, why? Was there provocation?

The role of the trade unions

Listening with a third ear

Although a trade union representative will invariably defend his member, his sympathy may be limited where he knows that the employee has genuinely committed misconduct. In these circumstances you may well be listening to a token defence. For example, no trade union official will ever knowingly say anything untrue in his member's defence. Consequently, phrases such as 'My member tells me' mean 'Believe him if you like'.

Plea bargaining

This is usually conducted on the basis of substituting a final warning for dismissal in return for a guarantee of no appeal. The choice is thus between the certainty of substantial disciplinary sanction against the possibility of dismissal as a more satisfactory but less certain outcome. The offer should be weighed against the strength of the case. How good is the evidence, how reliable are the witnesses, will the case be well presented? If there is a significant risk of a successful appeal, it might be wise to accept.

Trade unions walk out of hearing

Rarely does this happen where experienced officials are involved. Even where industrial relations are tense, the chance of conflict erupting is reduced where a thorough investigation has taken place, the case is thoroughly documented and the hearing is conducted in an orderly fashion and an appropriate atmosphere.

However, if the trade unions do withdraw from the hearing it is legally permissible to proceed — there is no breach of natural justice as the employee's side have been afforded the opportunity to hear the case against them and to respond. In law, they must accept the consequences of declining to participate. From the standpoint of managing industrial relations however, it may be wise to be patient and rearrange the hearing. If this option is adopted it should be made clear to the employee's side that this is a goodwill gesture and that the reconvened hearing will proceed regardless of whether the employee attends. If dismissal is a possible outcome, this should be stated.

Evaluating the evidence

A systematic approach to evaluation

Once the hearing is finished, everyone except the chairperson and his adviser, if he has one, withdraw. (Incidentally should it be necessary to recall one of the parties, both should be recalled otherwise bias may be claimed.)

The chairperson must now evaluate the evidence and decide what action, if any, to take. The evaluation is critical to the fairness of the decision. It must therefore be carried out rigorously and should never be rushed. If necessary, the hearing should be reconvened for another day in order to announce the decision.

Evaluation should be approached systematically as follows:

- Summarise the evidence for and against each accusation.

- Weigh each piece of evidence.

- Draw conclusions based on the balance of probabilities.

Summarising the evidence

Even the shortest of hearings is likely to generate copious notes. First, order these and then extract the evidence. A good method is to:

1. Use a highlighter pen to identify points of evidence.
2. Work through the notes, writing out the evidence for management on one half of a separate sheet.
3. Work back through the notes for the employee's side on the other half of the sheet.

4.   If necessary, repeat the process to summarise the evidence.

The following case shows how to apply this process. The sections marked in italic highlight the actual evidence.

An assistant in an old peoples' home was *accused of stealing money from a resident. Management's case* rested on the fact that *when the loss was discovered, the hands of all staff on duty were examined under ultra violet light. Traces of special dye on notes planted by the police showed on the employee's hands.*

The *employee denied* having any *contact* whatsoever *with the money.* The employee's trade union representative argued that the accusation was outrageous. The investigation had been appalling in that certain staff *present when the money had been stolen had been off duty at the time of the discovery* and their *hands were not checked.* Furthermore, none of the residents' hands had been checked.

The next step is to set out the evidence for and against:

- Management:
  — coincidence of dye.

- Employee:
  — investigation inadequate because:
  not all staff examined;
  no residents examined.

In this case it is unnecessary to summarise the evidence any further. The next step is to weigh the case for and the case against.

Evaluating the evidence

Evaluation involves two stages:

1.   Was the investigation adequate?
2.   If so, what is the reliability and significance of each piece of evidence?

The case of the stolen money referred to above fails the first question. The investigation is clearly inadequate in that the hands of all persons who could have had access to the money should have been examined. Interestingly forensic tests subsequently showed the reaction was caused by washing powder.

The reliability of evidence depends on factors such as the extent of corroboration, whether it is hearsay and if so, whether the hearsay is first-, second- or third-hand. An old police saying is 'An alibi is like virginity. If a bit of it's gone, all of it's gone'.

The balance of probabilities

Disciplinary hearings are ultimately decided on the balance of probability. Assessing the balance of probabilities entails comparing the evidence for and the evidence against. Look at the case below.

A candidate was accused of cheating in an examination. He had been caught with notes pencilled in minuscle handwriting on the back of a chewing gum wrapper. The candidate, however, insisted that they were revised notes brought into the examination room by accident.

Which of the two sides is the most probable? The fact that the notes were written on a chewing gum wrapper in a highly concentrated fashion is inconsistent with their being revision aids and consistent with deception. Therefore, it is more probable than not that the candidate was cheating.

Often the probabilities are much more finely balanced:

An employee was accused of failing to attend paid day-release sessions at college, the implication being that he spent the time at home or somewhere other than work. Management's evidence was based on a tutor's report which attributed the employee's examination failure to poor class attendance.

The tutor was unable to state exactly how many sessions the employee had missed but said it was at least 30 per cent. The employee said he had found the lectures poor and uninteresting and had therefore spent the time working in the library. He attributed his examination results to poor tuition.

There is no dispute that the employee missed some classes. Everything turns on whether he was at the library or elsewhere. On the one hand, there was a library and so he could well have used it. It is also possible that the tuition was poor. Equally, knowing that no proper registers were kept, the employee might have seen the opportunity to miss a few sessions and taken it. Certainly his examination results hardly suggest diligence. The weighing is so slight, however, that it seems reasonable to give the employee the benefit of the doubt though with the proviso that henceforth, he must attend all classes.

The next case is even more difficult.

A joiner was accused of gross misconduct for throwing a window frame out of a block of flats instead of carrying it down to the disposal van.

The joiner said that the window had slipped while he was removing it and he had to let go to stop himself from falling out of the window.

The best advice here might be to issue a warning for carelessness.

Deciding upon an appropriate penalty

The penalty should be based upon:

- the nature of the offence; and
- how similar cases have been dealt with in the past.

And also take into account:

- the employee's previous record; and
- any statement in mitigation.

We now discuss how each of these factors should be evaluated.

The nature of the offence

Much has been said in this book about the importance of trust and confidence in employer and employee relations. If this relationship has been destroyed, dismissal will normally be upheld. For example:

A senior manager responsible for cleaning services invited tenders for a supply of bin liners. Only one was received and it was duly accepted by the manager. It was subsequently discovered that the bags could have been purchased more cheaply from a supermarket and that the supplier happened to live next door to the manager.

Although there is no proof that the manager had received a secret profit, the employer felt he could no longer trust the manager. Dismissal might therefore have been a reasonable response. The manager clearly thought so because he resigned.

Not all serious disciplinary offences, however, destroy trust.

An education officer received an anonymous letter alleging that the headteacher of a special residential school had presented one of the boys with a picture of his favourite film star in scant attire as a reward for some extra work in the school garden. The presentation was made in front of all the pupils, and as the headteacher handed the boy the picture, he made a gesture indicating masturbation.

Ostensibly, here is a dismissal case. The headteacher was immediately suspended pending an investigation. This revealed that the boy concerned lacked confidence and had a poor self-image. The gift and accompanying gesture were intended to boost his standing with the group. The headteacher accepted that, with hindsight, it was inappropriate but had acted in the boy's best interests. Since in the light of this explanation the employer still retained confidence in the headteacher, he received only a final warning.

The nature of the offence is also relevant in deciding between dismissal and a final warning, and in deciding between a final or a written warning. In the case of the former, the critical question is, can I afford for the employee to repeat this offence? In the case of the latter, if the employee were to repeat the offence, would I be prepared to warn him again? A negative answer in both instances suggests the more severe option is appropriate.

Precedent and consistency

Discipline must be applied consistently. Rarely, however, are two cases identical. Careful analysis is, therefore, required to identify similarities and differences between cases.

Case 1

An order was placed for the manufacture of a metal gate. The workshop gang, however, were aware that there was an old gate lying in the yard which could easily be made serviceable. The foreman became suspicious when the gang claimed the full time for manufacturing the gate on their bonus returns when no material had been drawn from stores.

Case 2

A joiner was sent to replace a door. He found, however, that once shaved down, the old one hung perfectly. To boost his bonus earnings he booked the job as 'Replace Door'. He too was discovered because no door had been drawn from stores.

These two cases are virtually identical instances of mis-booking work and should therefore attract the same penalty with due account taken of length of service, factors in mitigation and so forth.

The next two cases concern misuse of vans but there are important differences between them:

Case 1

An employee decided to use a company van to visit home during his lunch break. Unfortunately, he had an accident and injured a woman pedestrian. He returned to site and immediately reported what had happened.

Case 2

An employee took a van out at lunch time. He collided with a car and drove off. During the afternoon he deliberately rammed the van into a school wall to disguise his earlier accident. He was discovered because the van's number plate had been noted at the scene of both incidents.

In the first case the employee is guilty of one allegation only, that is using the van without permission. Analysis of the second case, however, reveals multiple offences, namely:

- Using the van without permission.

- Failing to comply with the requirements of the Road Traffic Act 1972 at the scene of the collision.

- Causing deliberate damage to the van.

- Dishonesty over how the damage occurred.

Clearly then, the second case is substantially more serious than the first and should therefore attract a higher penalty. Interestingly, it was discovered in the first case that the employee had no driving licence despite having been employed as a 'stand-in' driver for two years. A veil was drawn over this at the disciplinary hearing!

Employee's previous record and evidence in mitigation

No definitive rules exist on how far these factors should be taken into account. Generally speaking the longer an employee's service and the more exemplary his record, the more these should moderate the disciplinary penalty.

The most unusual plea in mitigation I know of concerned a lorry driver about to be sacked for carrying passengers in his cab. It was claimed that his wooden leg had become infested with woodworm and that if he were to be dismissed he could not afford a replacement.

Again, generally speaking, genuine evidence in mitigation should moderate the disciplinary penalty. For example, an employee failing to observe a safety regulation said that he had been extremely tired because his wife was dangerously ill. In another instance the penalty for poor workmanship was reduced because the employee had been required to work under exceptional pressure.

The law recognises, however, that some disciplinary offences are so serious that dismissal is the only option, regardless of any of the foregoing factors. The main thing is that the employer is able to demonstrate that these were considered.

Totting up of warnings

The whole basis of a warning is against a person's future conduct and therefore it is quite common for someone to receive a warning for lateness followed by a second warning for bad language followed by a third and final warning for absence without permission or for any combination of offences.

Can expired warnings be taken into account?

ACAS recommends that disciplinary warnings do not remain upon an employee's file indefinitely and therefore most disciplinary procedures specify expiry dates. It is advisable, however, to retain some record of the warning, though it should only be referred to if:

● the employee claims he has an exemplary record; or

● there is evidence that he is abusing the disciplinary system by committing further misconduct immediately upon the expiry of a warning.

Implementing disciplinary action

The decision should be delivered verbally in the presence of both parties. The following checklist indicates the points to be covered.

Checklist for implementing disciplinary action

1. Recapitulate the allegations.
2. State your conclusions in respect of each allegation.
3. Explain how you have reached these conclusions.
4. Summarise your findings.
5. State what sanction, if any, you intend to impose.
6. (If appropriate, mention any training or assistance the organisation can offer the employee.)
7. (If appropriate, indicate that any further misconduct will result in more serious disciplinary action or dismissal if the decision results in a final warning.)
8. Inform the employee of his rights of appeal.

The decision should then be confirmed in writing. The letter or memo should incorporate all the points set out in the checklist as follows:

Dear

This is to confirm the Disciplinary Hearing held in my office on Tuesday 4 November attended by Mr Philips the group manager and Mr Harwood the personnel officer. You were represented by Mr Logan of the TGWU.

(1) → The purpose of the hearing was to consider an allegation that you have breached your contract by undertaking outside employment during working hours.

(2) → Having listened to the case put by management and Mr Logan's representations on your behalf, I find the allegation substantiated.

(3) → This conclusion is based on the evidence of sickness records which show that you and your colleague Mr Brown have had almost identical periods of absence over the past 18 months amounting to 74 days all

taken during periods of fine weather. This evidence is consistent with working as a team on outside contracts. Therefore, despite your denial, I conclude on the balance of probabilities that you have undertaken outside work while drawing sick pay.

4 → I regard this as gross misconduct.

5 → I have therefore decided in view of your previous final warning, to dismiss you with immediate effect.

8 → You have ten days in which to appeal against my decision and can exercise this right by writing to the director (Design and Build) of the Northern Counties Division.

Yours sincerely

As with all disciplinary communications, this letter is composed with appeals panels and industrial tribunals in mind. Listing those present not only provides useful background information for those unfamiliar with the organisation, but it is also a means of demonstrating that the case was heard in accordance with the organisation's disciplinary procedure including the fact that the employee was properly represented. Where representation is declined, the letter should reflect this.

The phrase 'having listened' emphasises that both sides of the story have been put and that natural justice has been observed in that the employee clearly knew the case against him and his explanation has been heard. The rationale for the decision is clear. Where the employee's previous record or length of service has resulted in a lesser penalty being imposed this should be stated. Avoid expressions such as 'deep regret' in composing letters of dismissal as these may be taken to imply that dismissal was unnecessary and therefore unfair.

Summary dismissal is appropriate in cases of gross misconduct. Notice may be afforded where persistent minor misconduct has led to dismissal. Employees dismissed in these circumstances customarily receive pay in lieu of notice in the interests of removing them from the workplace. This is not obligatory however.

A final warning should include a statement that no further warnings will be given.

A copy of this letter will be placed on your file for one year, after which it will be expunged from the record. I warn you that any further misconduct will result in dismissal. No more warnings will be given.

Warnings should be phrased 'further, more serious disciplinary action will follow'.

Time limit for lodging an internal appeal

This applies from the date of the hearing. It is courtesy to supply written confirmation within a day or two if possible. In any case, full-time employees with six months' service may request a written statement of reasons for dismissal and employers are legally obliged to respond within two weeks unless not reasonably practicable. Summary dismissal and the commencement of the notice also take effect from the date of the hearing.

Procedure for an appeal

The stages involved in preparation and presentation of an appeal are the same as for a disciplinary hearing. The same rules of natural justice and so forth apply (see Chapter One). Potential grounds for an appeal are perhaps one, or a combination of, the following:

- The original hearing was conducted unfairly.

- The facts of the case are in dispute.

- Important evidence in the employee's favour was not taken into account.

- The penalty imposed was too severe.

- The penalty imposed was inconsistent with the organisation's response to similar offences.

- Mitigating factors were not fully taken into account.

- The emergence of new evidence.

The decision, which can only either reduce or uphold the penalty, should be announced verbally at the hearing and subsequently confirmed in writing. It is good practice to give detailed reasons for the decision as a means of demonstrating that procedures have been correctly applied. As a guide, the document should contain the same level of detail as used in warning or dismissal letters. A similar format may also be used.

Supporting a subordinate's decision

An appeal should always be decided on its merits. It is a mistake to uphold an unsatisfactory case out of misplaced loyalty to a subordinate since the likelihood is that it will only be overturned later and after additional time and expense. Moreover, protecting a subordinate in this way is counter-productive as he is denied the opportunity to learn from his mistakes.

Summary and checklist

- The purposes of a disciplinary hearing are to decide whether a case exists against the employee and if so, the appropriate level of action if any.

- The chairperson is responsible for ensuring that hearings are conducted in accordance with the rules of natural justice and in an orderly and efficient manner.

- An essential skill in chairing hearings is to combine formality and flexibility. If in doubt, err on the side of the employee.

- Where the employer has a strong case, common defence strategies include attacking management, mitigation, confusion and minimisation.

- Fairness requires a systematic approach to decision making.

- It is essential to be able to explain *how* and *why* a particular decision has been reached.

- In deciding, how have you taken into account:
  - the nature of the offence;
  - precedent;
  - factors in mitigation?

- The decision should be announced promptly but not at the expense of allowing adequate time to consider.

- An internal appeal is essentially a repeat of the disciplinary hearing.

- Appeals must be conducted to the same standard of fairness and methodological rigour as disciplinary hearings.

- It is advisable to confirm an appeal decision in writing, and in the same detail as a warning or dismissal letter.

- Appeal decisions must be made on their merits. They should never reflect loyalty to a subordinate.

Chapter Sixteen
Going to an Industrial Tribunal

Introduction

Industrial tribunal procedure is outside the scope of this book which is concerned with management of workplace discipline. If the practices and procedures set out in the preceding chapters have been properly applied, dismissed employees' prospects of success at a tribunal are minimal. It is appreciated, however, that this represents the ideal state, and in any case, an employee has nothing to lose by applying to have his case heard. The following notes are intended as general guidance only. The reader is advised to consult specialist sources if detailed information is required.

The tribunal system

The purpose of a tribunal

Tribunals exist to provide a cheap, speedy and informal facility for adjudicating minor industrial cases. They were first established in 1964 to hear appeals against training levy assessments, and the scope of their jurisdiction has since expanded to encompass a great deal of industrial legislation. This includes time off for trade union duties, public duties and antenatal care; guarantee payments, redundancy, unfair discrimination, contributions to pension schemes, trade union ballots, expulsion from trade union membership and wages, as well as unfair dismissal.

The original intention of the tribunal system was to dispense with court formality by providing a plain-sense approach to disputes where parties could present their own cases without the trouble and expense of requiring legal representation. Although the proliferation of legislation and case law has eroded the tribunals' freedom from legality, they remain relatively informal. For example, they are exempt from court rules on the admissibility of evidence. Moreover, it is still quite realistic for parties to represent themselves. Representation is equally acceptable, for example, by solicitor or barrister, a trade union official or the Citizen's Advice Bureau.

Composition of tribunals

Tribunals consist of three members:

1. A legally qualified chairperson.
2. A lay person representing employers' organisations.
3. A lay person representing employees' organisations.

The purpose of representation is to enable members to contribute their respective experience to decisions. All members of the tribunal, however, are expected to adjudicate impartially and to observe the law. The chairperson is of equal status to the other two members. Decisions may be by a majority vote, even where the chairperson dissents.

Processing appeals

Appealing to a tribunal

Employers are not obliged to notify employees of any right of appeal to a tribunal or how to exercise it. The onus is upon the employee to initiate the application. Cases typically originate by an employee or ex-employee submitting what is known as a *Form IT1* to a local tribunal office. Alternatively, an appeal can be lodged by letter providing it contains all the information required by the form. The requisite information includes details such as the *applicant's* (as the employee is known) name and address, and an outline of the basis of their case.

Time limit for lodging an appeal

This varies according to the nature of the appeal. The limit for unfair dismissal claims is *three months from the effective date of termination*. In other words, from the original date of dismissal. Time limits tend to be strictly enforced. Dismissed employees are therefore advised to apply immediately without awaiting the outcome of an internal appeal.

Replying to a claim

Employers are formally notified of claims via a document known as the *IT2*. As *respondent*, the employer is required to *reply within 14 days* on form *IT3*. Respondents automatically receive copies of the originating application (Form IT1). Respondents are required to indicate whether they:

- intend to resist the application; and
- if so, on what grounds?

Basis for a defence

Respondents must clearly indicate the reason for dismissal. Within the context of employee discipline admissible reasons for dismissal are on the basis of the employee's:

- capability of qualifications;
- conduct; or
- some other substantial reason of a kind such as to justify dismissal.

Respondents are further required to explain the full grounds for dismissal. No precise requirements exist as to format but the explanation should normally include the following information:

- Previous warnings (where relevant).
- Statement of the facts of the case.
- The justification for dismissal.

The time limit for replying may be extended if the tribunal is satisfied that good cause exists. Employers are urged to reply promptly, however, as any failure to enter an appearance (ie return the form) debars the respondent from participating in proceedings. In other words, failure to reply within the 14-day limit can cost you the case. Either side may subsequently seek permission to amend the so-called 'Notice of Appearance'.

Pre-hearing review

This is a mechanism whereby cases with no obvious prospect of success can be prevented from proceeding to a full hearing.

Witness orders

Tribunals can compel the attendance of any persons as witness wherever they may be within the UK. This is similar to the power of subpoena and is normally only exercised where a prospective witness's evidence is potentially critical or where it is necessary to enforce attendance.

Striking out

Tribunals can decline to hear cases which are obviously scandalous, vexatious or frivolous, or what is known as 'want of prosecution'. Want of prosecution means inordinate, disrespectful delay in pursuing the case. Striking out may also be ordered where there is a serious possibility that justice to the employer may be prejudiced because of inexcusable delay.

Settlement and withdrawal

Either side may offer to settle the case before it is heard by the tribunal either through personal negotiation or via the ACAS conciliation officer. A settlement can be reached as late as in the waiting room immediately before the case is heard. Furthermore, where a tribunal finds against an employer, there may be an opportunity to settle compensation privately.

Preparing for a hearing

Unless the parties agree otherwise, they are entitled to a minimum of 14 days' notice of a hearing. The preparation needed for presenting a case is similar to that for a disciplinary hearing outlined in previous chapters with the following additional points:

- Ensure all witnesses are notified of the hearing. If an important witness is unable to attend, apply at once for a postponement.

- Documents should be paginated and include a contents list and a brief summary. Six identical copies are required.

- If possible agree a bundle of documents with the other side.

- Large bundles of documentation should be submitted in advance to allow the tribunal time to familiarise themselves with the contents.

- Where appropriate, it is useful if documents contain reference to specific cases or points of law.

Addressing an industrial tribunal

Again, similar comments to those for presenting disciplinary cases apply though with more force. Key points to bear in mind are that the panel:

- knows nothing about your organisation;

- will need to take detailed notes;

- concentrates intensely;

- can only adjudicate upon what it hears on the day.

In addressing the panel therefore, it is essential to:

- Speak clearly and at a pace slow enough for detailed notes to be taken.

- Pause periodically to ensure that the panel is following you.

- Explain background information concisely and clearly.

- Avoid jargon; if it is necessary to use technical terms explain them to the panel.

Initial formalities

On arrival you will be shown into the respondents' waiting room. The applicants wait in a separate room. The clerk will conduct you to the room where the hearing is to be held. The respondent sits on the right of the room, the applicant on the left. Witnesses sit at the back of the room. They may come and go as required. Everyone is asked to stand as the tribunal enters the room and remain standing until the chairperson asks everyone to sit. Address the chairperson as 'Sir' or 'Madam'. Proceedings are conducted sitting.

Hearings are open to the public, though in certain circumstances, a hearing *in camera* can be arranged.

Opening the proceedings

In unfair dismissal cases, the tribunal's first task is to establish whether there has been a dismissal. Where dismissal is admitted, usually the chairperson will outline the procedure and then invite the employer to open by explaining the reason for the dismissal.

Presenting a case

The procedure at an industrial tribunal is similar to the model for a disciplinary hearing shown on page 233, with the exception of the opening statement. The right to make an opening statement has been abolished and is now at the tribunal's discretion. Permission may be granted where the case is legally or factually complex. If permitted, the address must be confined to a brief synopsis of:

- the case itself;

- the evidence to be presented;

- any legal issues arising.

An opening statement is not given on oath and therefore is not officially noted.

Giving evidence

If presenting a case in person, it is advisable to read from a pre-prepared statement. Witnesses, however, are normally only allowed to refer to notes to refresh their memory. The procedure for referring to documents is for the witness to be asked to identify the document and to read aloud the relevant points, piece by piece. Presenters are not normally allowed to undertake this task themselves.

The tribunal usually ask questions at the end of the respective cross-examinations although they may seek clarification at any point. It is important to listen carefully to the nature and direction of questions as these may yield a clue as to how the case is viewed and what issues should be emphasised.

If the applicant is unrepresented, the chairperson may ask a great many questions. This does not constitute bias, it is simply a means of ensuring the relevant points are expressed and that justice is thereby done.

Objections

Either side or the chairperson may object during the proceedings. It is permissible and obviously sensible to argue against an objection if there are grounds for doing so. If overruled, accept with good grace. In court it is customary to say 'I am obliged to you'. For the purposes of a tribunal, a simple 'thank you' will suffice.

If the chairperson interrupts unduly or otherwise behaves impatiently or unfairly, you can ask for the difficulty to be 'noted on record'. In extreme circumstances, it is possible to ask the panel to stand down on grounds of having lost confidence in them.

Adjournments

Tribunals are usually willing to grant short adjournments to enable either side to reassemble its case, enquire after a witness and so forth. Longer adjournments which involve re-convening on another day can involve costs.

Decision

At the end of the hearing, the panel retire. The decision may be announced in full, or the announcement may consist of the decision only, with reasons to follow. Sometimes the tribunal will need time to consider the issues, in which case judgement is reserved and usually conveyed by post. All decisions are confirmed in writing with detailed reasons. Costs are only awarded in exceptional circumstances.

Tribunals and small employers

Small employers are largely exempt from adherance to rigorous standards of evidence and presentation. The main points to remember are:

- You are simply required to explain what happened and why you dismissed the employee.

- The chairperson will guide you.

A good way to prepare is to write out a short address containing the following points.

Checklist for presenting a case to a tribunal for a small employer

- Your name.

- Brief details about your business including:
  — numbers employed;
  — administrative resources (if none exist it is important to say so).

- How long the dismissed employee worked for you and in what capacity.

- A brief description of the employee's duties.

- An explanation of what took place including:
  — dates;
  — times;
  — places;
  — witnesses (if any); and
  — who said what, and to who.

For example:

1. My name is Peter Smith.
2. I run a small welding and engineering shop in Peterborough. I employ 25 staff besides myself. I have one part-time clerk to help with the wages and other paper work.
3. George Porter worked for me for three years as a foreman.
4. He is responsible for dealing with customers when I am busy or out.
5. On Monday 2 July at about half past three I heard a row going on in the yard and saw George Porter shake his fist at a customer. I ran

towards them and heard George Porter say 'Any more of that and I'll flatten you'. I told George Porter to go into the office and wait. The customer said that the row started because a job had not been finished on time. He was very upset. After he had left the yard I asked George Porter what had happened. He said the customer had sworn at him. I said that was no excuse for threatening violence and that I would have to sack him because I can't afford to lose customers.

Summary and checklist

- Tribunals exist to provide cheap and speedy access to justice with the minimum of formality.

- Tribunals consist of three members, one professional and two lay. All are of equal status.

- The onus of lodging an appeal rests with the employee.

- The time limit for responding to notification of an appeal (Form IT3), is 14 days. Failure to observe this time limit can cost the case.

- On Form IT3, the employer must indicate the reason for dismissal and the basis of the case.

- Either side may offer to settle a claim privately.

- The requirements for preparing and presenting a case are similar to those for a discplinary hearing. Bear in mind, however, that the tribunal know nothing about your organisation.

- Witnesses are required to give evidence with minimal reliance upon notes.

- It is customary for witnesses to relate documentary evidence.

- Tribunals are required to act impartially and observe the law. It is possible to have a difficulty noted or even to ask the panel to stand down.

- The decision may be announced orally on the day or conveyed in writing at a later date. All decisions are confirmed in writing.

Index